Community Dances Manual

Books 1–7

Series Editor: Douglas Kennedy
in association with
The English Folk Dance
and Song Society

ENGLISH FOLK DANCE AND SONG SOCIETY

1949, 1954, 1957, 1964, 1967 by
the English Folk Dance and Song Society
1986 by Princeton Book Company, Publishers
P.O. Box 109, Princeton, NJ 08542
© 1991 The English Folk
Dance and Song Society, 2 Regent's Park Road,
London NW1 7AY
ISBN 0 85418 155 5
Cover art by Karen Brown
Cover design by BACKES Graphic Productions
Reproduced and printed by Halstan & Co. Ltd.,
Amersham, Bucks., England

Contents

NEW FEATURES

- The entire original text is included
- Larger, easy-to-read format
- Spiral binding opens flat
- New Introduction by Tony Parkes
- Dance and tune indices
- Up-to-date bibliography and discography
- All-in-one format—More economical to purchase, easier to use
- More complete dance step glossary
- Sample dance programmes

This complete, unabridged republication of THE COMMUNITY DANCES MANUALS, originally published as 7 separate books by the English Folk Dance and Song Society, brings together 130 of the most popular dances performed at today's contra, square, and social dances. Complete, easy-to-follow instructions give the caller, at a glance, all of the information needed to quickly teach and prompt a dance. On a facing page, the appropriate music (with guitar chords) is printed for use by the musicians. These dances have been tested by hundreds of callers in schools, churches, town halls, gymnasiums—wherever people gather to enjoy an evening of dance.

ABOUT THE AUTHORS

DOUGLAS KENNEDY is one of the founders of the English folk dance movement, along with Cecil Sharp and Maud Karpeles. He has collected song and dance throughout the British Isles, and published extensively in folklore and popular journals. He compiled this book with the aid of his son, Peter, and British dance scholars Michael Bell, Jack Hamilton, and American dancer/caller Ralph Page.

TONY PARKES is a New England-based caller of squares and contra dances. Since 1964, he has presented traditional dancing in schools, churches, social clubs, and community centers to people of all ages and all levels of experience. He has written many original dances and made several recordings, including an album with calls, *KITCHEN JUNKET* (Alcazar Records), and he performs regularly with the band Yankee Ingenuity.

OF RELATED INTEREST

Series of 12″ LP records available from the folk shop. C.D.M. 1-7.
To provide music for steps described in this book.
Cassette TC EMS 1387 (EMI)

Introduction

THIS book is a compilation of seven collections of English and American country dances, originally published between 1949 and 1967 by the English Folk Dance and Song Society, London. They have seen wide and continued use on both sides of the Atlantic, and will be even more welcome in this new and larger format.

Some of the circle, square, and longways dances given here are "traditional" in the generally accepted sense: They were collected in the field from communities that had been dancing them for generations. Others were devised by callers and teachers working with many types of recreational groups, combining existing figures to meet various needs. But all of the dances stand solidly in the Anglo-American tradition. For the most part, they are fairly easy, with only a handful of terms to memorize. And they are indeed community dances, emphasizing group over partner interaction—though there is plenty of opportunity to enjoy one's partner!

A few points should be made here, especially to those encountering the dances for the first time:

- Country dancing at its best requires a delicate balance of individual freedom within a team structure. This can only be realized through actually dancing, leading, or playing the music. Beginners are unlikely to get the feel of the dance right away, but they should keep that goal in mind. They will learn much faster in company with experienced dancers. If at all possible, leaders unfamiliar with these forms (and perhaps a few key dancers from their groups) should visit communities where the dances have been done for some time.

- There is no single "right" way to perform any of these dances. Leaders and dancers have modified most of them over time—deliberately or accidentally, after much forethought or on the spot. An experienced leader can substitute a simpler figure for one that the group may not know or might have trouble grasping. But new leaders are advised to try the dances as given here before making any changes.

- The leader must set the tone of the dance: decorous but not stifling, informal but not rowdy. The ideal, even with a new group, is to teach without appearing to do so. This can be done by choosing material with care, introducing only one or two new figures or concepts with each dance. In general, the less talking, the better. Experience will show how a figure can be taught in a few words. Asking one set of two or three couples to demonstrate a movement can be helpful.

- "Calling," or prompting the movements during the dance, is not traditional for all of these dances, but it is certainly appropriate, especially with new dancers. In the New England contra dances, calling is part of the tradition, often becoming an art in itself. The calls are delivered in rhythm with the music but do not necessarily rhyme. Each call should end just before the phrase of music it refers to: The dancers should know what they are to do by the time the music tells them to do it. In other words, the music and not the caller dictates the timing of these dances (unlike traditional squares and circles in the Southern and Western US). As with other aspects of the dance, calling is best learned by example, at other callers' dances if possible, with records and tapes as a supplement or substitute.

- The music is of prime importance in making country dancing a success. It should be played with a light touch, emphasizing the upbeat, getting under the dancers' feet and lifting them up. Again, examples are almost essential for new dance musicians, even those who may be experienced players of other forms of music. Recordings are a great help in learning the tunes and style. Recorded music at dances is a poor substitute for good live music but can serve well while local musicians prepare to take over. Perhaps the band can play two or three numbers a night at first, working up to a full evening as their skill and confidence grow.

    Many of the tunes given here are easy to play; other easy tunes can be found in the books listed. Set dances generally have their own tune, but progressive longways (especially New England contras) may be done to any tune of the right length. The majority of dance tunes comprise 32 measures of $\frac{2}{4}$ (reel) or $\frac{6}{8}$ (jig) time. The usual pattern is an eight-measure "A part" which is played twice, followed by a "B part" which is also eight measures repeated. This is given in the notations as A.1.; A.2.; B.1.; B.2. Variations such as "C" or "D" parts or unusual repeats are noted.

- The Glossary may appear to contain more than the "handful of terms" mentioned earlier, but of the hundred-odd entries, only about two dozen are truly basic movements (the others are variants, starting formations, or alternative names). The original compilers of the Manuals intended their notations for users who already knew country dance terminology. The descriptions are therefore adequate for those who know the terms and mystifying to those who don't. Hence the length of the present glossary, which is meant to define any term about which there is likely to be any question. Note that many variations on the basic movements exist, too many to include here. If a particular variant is important to a dance, it is described in detail in the notation of that dance (see, for instance, the variant of "ladies chain" in "The Rifleman" or the directions for the "pousette" in "Foula Reel").

- The descriptions of American dances are good for the most part, but not always entirely accurate. In particular, it is not traditional to use an elbow swing in "turn contra corners." Note that this figure is mentioned under "Threesome Sicilians," but described without its usual name at "Chorus Jig" and "Sackett's Harbor," classic contra dances well-known for including it.

With these points in mind, relax and approach these dances for the joy they can bring to those who do them.

TONY PARKES

NOTE: I am indebted to Douglas Kennedy for many of the points covered here, which were mentioned in his introductions to the original volumes.

Sample Programmes

NOTE: Many dances are suitable for beginners and experienced dancers alike. These programmes are rather extreme examples of material appropriate for one or the other group.

SAMPLE PROGRAMME FOR BEGINNERS

1. Big Circle: "Big Set Mixer"
2. Longways Set Dance: "Galopede"
3. Big Circle: "Lucky Seven" or "Patacake Polka"
4. Threesome: "Three Meet" (progressive) or "Triple Promenade" (mixer)
5. Progressive Longways: "Fairfield Fancy"
6. Square: "Cumberland Square Eight"
7. Progressive Longways: "Haymakers' Jig"
8. Square: "Ninepins Quadrille"
9. Longways Set Dance: "Virginia Reel"
10. Progressive Circle: "Waltz Country Dance" (may be turned into a free waltz around the hall after a few rounds)

SAMPLE PROGRAMME FOR EXPERIENCED DANCERS

1. Progressive Longways: "Lady Walpole's Reel"
2. Big Circle: "Blaydon Races"
3. Progressive Longways: "Bonny Breast Knot" (Sussex)
4. Square: "La Russe"
5. Progressive Longways: "Road to California"
6. Big Circle: "Circle Waltz"
   (Interval)
7. Progressive Longways: "Morpeth Rant"
8. Progressive Circle: "Black Jack"
9. Longways Set Dance: "The Ploughboy"
10. Progressive Threesome: "Walpole Cottage"
11. Progressive Longways: "Sackett's Harbour"
12. Progressive Circle: "Margaret's Waltz"

1

COUNTRY DANCES suitable for indoor and out-of-door recreation with the description of fifteen dances and fifteen tunes.

Introduction

Edited by
Douglas Kennedy

THE recurring tendency to get together, so manifest on occasions of celebration, invariably expresses itself in some form of group dancing. Arm-in-arm or hand-in-hand, crowds will cheerfully mill around without any coherent plan or common aim. The old dance forms devised for celebration have been forgotten and need re-introducing. There is no need to invent new forms—in fact, it would be impossible to make up a form of group dance that hasn't already been invented for centuries. There are plenty of old forms that can be made to serve present-day requirements.

This manual is a selection of Community Dances chosen for their simplicity and suitability for present-day requirements. British in origin, some of them have been carried by our forefathers to America and Canada and preserved there. The Country Dances in themselves constitute a complete programme but they can be combined with the Square Dances " called " in American fashion, and with Old-time Couple Dances to give the programme a wider application.

The description given of each dance is just sufficient to enable an M.C. to present the dance and to guide the dancers through the first tentative steps. It presupposes a knowledge of the style and manner of set dancing and of the steps that can be used.

More important than the dance-descriptions are the traditional dance melodies, on the playing of which the whole success of Community Dancing depends. Some of these melodies are attached to particular dance figures but most of them can be used at will for a whole heap of dances. The vital factor is rhythm. The bands that play these old dance airs must find the proper way to play them so that they lift the dancers along.

Apart from the music, the successful Community Dance depends upon the " Caller " or M.C. He it is who must set the atmosphere of cheerful informality. He must present a vivid picture of the dance movement and shepherd his dancers into the figures without too much ordering about. In the Square Dances the " calling " is an art in itself but even in the simple figure dances it is advisable to keep up a certain amount of calling until the company as a whole has picked up the figure sequence and settled down to real dance enjoyment.

The ideal company of dancers for community dancing is one composed of equal numbers of men and girls. The aim is to promote the maximum of individual freedom of movement within the requirements of team-work. This needs a nice adjustment of social give and take, only to be acquired through set-dance experience.

So let the band strike up and create a cheerful atmosphere. The M.C. calls for a few couples who know the first dance to show the general plan. He assembles the company, starts it off and " calls " each part of the figure until everyone has got the whole idea. They can then be left to discover the further delights of community dancing.

DOUGLAS KENNEDY.

1. LA RUSSE QUADRILLE

(As danced in the Border villages,
collected by Peter Kennedy.)

(The first four bars of the tune are played as an introduction.)

Music: "La Russe" or any reel.

Form: A square set of four couples.

A.1.   Man moves behind partner to the girl on the right, who moves to meet him. All balance and swing.

A.2.   Men return to partners, balance and swing.

B.1.   Leading couple swing.

B.2.   Leading couple then promenade inside the set to places.

A.3.   Leading couple crosses over with opposite couple (passing inside). Partners change places. Cross back in the same way (opposite couple passing inside).

A.4.   Repeat the cross over figure.

B.3.   All join hands and circle left.

B.4.   Promenade partners to places.

The movements are then repeated, each couple in turn leading.

2. SPANISH WALTZ (A Waltz Quadrille)

(As danced in the Border villages,
collected by Peter Kennedy.)

Music: "My lodging is on the cold ground" or any 32 bar waltz.

Form: A square set for four couples.

A.   All join hands and balance forward and back, then the men pass their left hand girl into their partner's place. Repeat three times.

B.   All waltz once round the set (ball-room direction).

The movements are then repeated as often as desired.

The dance can also be danced in sets of five or more couples.

LA RUSSE

D.C. al Segno

MY LODGING IS ON THE COLD GROUND

'TWAS WITHIN A MILE

MORPETH RANT

SOLDIER'S JOY

3. CUMBERLAND LONG EIGHT

Music: " 'Twas within a mile ".
(Tune collected from Tom Moses, of Lanercost, Cumberland.)

Form: Long set of four couples.

A.1. First man followed by the other men, turns out and dances to the bottom of the set, while the girls do the same on their side. Partners meet and dance up the middle to places. (Double step.)

A.2. With crossed hands the first couple, followed by the others, turns out to the left, dances to the bottom of the set and up the middle to places.

B.1. First and second couples right and left hands across, while third and fourth couples do the same.

B.2. First couple swing down the middle of the set to the bottom, while the rest of the dancers move up.

4. MORPETH RANT
(Collected by Maud Karpeles)

Music: "Morpeth Rant" or any other rant tune.

Form: Longways duple proper.

A.1. First man turns contrary with right, gives left to her partner, facing up between second couple who face down.

Stepping, three-in-a-line, whilst first woman dances under both arches, passing round her partner.

A.2. Right hands across and left hands back (turning outward to change hands.)

B.1. First couple down centre and back. Second couple move up.

B.2. Couples polka swing around each other.

5. SOLDIER'S JOY
(Collected by Maud Karpeles)

Music: "Soldier's Joy" or any other rant tune.

Form: Longways duple proper.

A.1. First couple down outside and back to form a line of four with second couple, who face outward.

A.2. Reel of four and return to original places.

B.1. First couple down centre and back. Second couple move up.

B.2. Couples polka swing around each other.

6. PATACAKE POLKA

Music: "Nick Nack Paddy Whack", "Little Brown Jug", "Buffalo Girls".

Form: 2 concentric circles, men inside facing partners.

A. Ballroom hold: To man's left: heel, toe, heel, toe, 4 chassays. Repeat to right.

B. 3 claps each to partner's right, to partner's left, to partner's both hands, to own knees. Each man gives his girl a right arm swing and passes her on to a new partner as he moves one place to his left.

This dance exists in many variations.

The form and progression may be used for any sequence to suit the occasion, as a good mixer and to help beginners to get the feel of typical dance movements and partner-handling.

7. STEAM-BOAT (Devon)
(Collected by Maud Karpeles)

Music: "Steamboat" or any 32 bar hornpipe.

Form: Longways duple proper.
(First couple between second: link arms and face down.)

A.1. Four abreast down the room and back.

A.2. First couple (followed by second) down again, then turn back and under second's arch to original places.

B.1. Right and left hands across.

B.2. Couples swing and change.

8. THE CUMBERLAND REEL

Music: The Cumberland Reel, or any 32 bar reel or jig.

Form: Long Set for four, five or six couples.

A.1. Two top couples right hands across and left hands back.

A.2. First couple down centre and back, man cast left and partner right, others following.

B.1. First couple make arch at bottom, others promenade up centre.

B.2. All promenade round to left (followed by first couple).

9. THE SQUARE EIGHT (Cumberland)

Music: "My love she's but a lassie yet", or any 32 bar reel or jig.

Form: Square set of four couples.

A.1. & 2. Tops: galop across and back. Sides: the same.

B.1. & 2. Tops: right hands across and left hands back. Sides: the same.

A.1. & 2. Tops: form a basket. Sides: the same.

B.1. & 2. All join hands and circle left. Promenade partner to place.

LITTLE BROWN JUG

NICK NACK PADDY WHACK

STEAM-BOAT

MY LOVE SHE'S BUT A LASSIE

CAIRN ON THE MOOR

SHANDON BELLS

THERE' NAE LUCK ABOOT THE HOOSE

10. WALTZ COUNTRY DANCE

("The Guaracha" or "Spanish Dance" described in "The Ballroom", 1827.)

Music: "Cairn on the Moor" or any 40-bar waltz (or 32 bars plus 8-bar "waltz-on").

Form: Sicilian Circle.

A.1. & 2. Face opposites. Balance forward and back, forward and change places. Face partners and repeat. Repeat with opposites, and then with partners again.

B.1. & 2. Hands in a ring. Balance forward and back and change woman from left to right. Repeat movement (four times in all).

B.3. Waltz on to next couple.

11. WAVES OF TORY

(An American version of a dance of Irish origin.)

Music: Any jig, such as "Shandon Bells", played A-A-B-B-A-B.

Form: Longways for five couples.

A.1. Lines forward and back, then form right hand stars to place, bottom couple right hand turn.

A.2. As A.1 with left hand stars, etc.

B.1. Top couple galop down and back.

B.2. They cast left and right, making arch at bottom to let following couples through.

A.3. & B.3. Complete circuit of Dip and Dive. Bottom couple (previous leaders) face up, others down. All take partner's inside hand. Progressive under and over, led by bottom couple going under. Couples on reaching end of set turn toward each other and return under and over, etc.

12. THADY YOU GANDER OR IRISH TROT

Music: "There's nae luck aboot the hoose" or any other suitable tune.

Form: Longways set for four couples.

A.1. First man leads partner down the middle below the fourth couple, crosses over with her and both come up on the outside of the set, the man on the girl's side and the girl on the man's side.

A.2. First girl, followed by second, third and fourth men, dances round the girl's side and back to places.

A.3. First man, followed by second, third and fourth girl, dances round the men's side and back to places.

B.1. & 2. "Strip the willow" figure. First couple arm left, then each dancer arms right with next-door contrary partner, meeting again in the middle of set to arm left with own partner, and repeating the movement, arming with each couple in turn until they reach the bottom of the set. The figure is repeated by the second, third and fourth couple in turn.

13. THE CIRCASSIAN AND THE BIG CIRCLE
   (Collected by Maud Karpeles in Northumberland)

Music: A jig tune for one part and a reel for the other.

PART 1: The Circassian Circle

Form: Sicilian Circle.

A.1. Right and left through or girls cross over (left) and men cross over (right), and repeat to places.

A.2. Partners balance and swing.

B.1. Ladies Chain.

B.2. Swing and change *OR* Promenade on to next couple.

PART 2: The Big Circle

Form: All join hands in one ring: Each man with his partner on his right facing centre.

A.1. Forward and back twice.

A.2. Girls to centre and back again.
Men go in and back to contrary partner, i.e. the girl on his left.

B.1. Swing her round.

B.2. Promenade around.

14. VIRGINIA REEL

Music: Jigs or Reels. ("Turkey in the Straw")

Form: Longways set for four or five couples.

In the normal version the opening sequence of movements involves only the corner dancers. The "family" version requires all the dancers to perform them simultaneously with their partners.

Lines advance and retire (twice).

Single turn with right hand—then with left hand.

Turn with both hands—then back to back (passing by the right).

Top couple only, galop down the sets and back again.

"Strip the Willow" by 1st couple, turning each other with right arm and contrary partners with left arm, working down the set to the bottom.

1st couple galop back to the top of the set and cast off, man to the left and partner to the right, followed by the other couples.

1st couple make an arch at the bottom of the set and the other dancers led by the 2nd couple move through the arch to the top of the set.

Movements repeated with 2nd couple in the lead, then with 3rd couple and so on.

THE IRISH WASHERWOMAN

MISS McLEOD'S REEL

TURKEY IN THE STRAW

15. THREE MEET (or The Swedish) (Gloucestershire)
   (Collected by Clare Newhouse)

Music: Three Meet or any 32 bar jig.

Form: One man with two partners facing another three, in circle round the room.

A.1. Threes take hands, forward and back, forward and cross over.

A.2. Repeat to places.

B.1. Circle six left and right.

B.2. Rings of three, swing and change places (progression).

2

COUNTRY DANCES suitable for indoor and out-of-door recreation with the description of eighteen dances and seventeen tunes.

1. BELFAST DUCK

(Arranged by Douglas Kennedy for Community Dancing)

Music: The Belfast Hornpipe or any other hornpipe.

Form: Progressive Longways contra: man facing partner (hands four).
(Warning 1st couples to make arch when the duck comes.)

A. Circle around to the left and back the other way.

B. Men lead partners with inside hand (for one bar), with both hands (for one bar).

Down 2, Sidestep 2, Up 2, Sidestep 2
Down 2, Sidestep 2. Arch.
Second couple duck under arch made by first.

2. HUNT THE SQUIRREL (Surrey)

(Collected by Cecil Sharp – Country Dance Book 1 – and included by permission of Messrs. Novello & Co.)

Music: "Hunt the Squirrel" or any other hornpipe.

Form: Progressive Longways: man facing girl (four handed sets).

A.1. Hands four to the left and back.

B.1. First couple lead down, turn and lead back to face second couple, who move up.

A.2. Second and first couples facing, move down the set. As they come back the second couples make an arch for first couples to dance through – all back in places.

B.2. First and second couples swing and change (double step).

3. HULL'S VICTORY

Music: "Hull's Victory" or any lively reel.

Form: Progressive Longways: man facing girl (four handed sets).

A.1.   First man half turn partner with right hand and both stand between second couple, four in a line, men face down and girls up. Balance right and left and elbow swing with contraries twice round.

A.2.   First man full turn partner right hand into the same line of four. Balance right and left. First couple swing in the centre of set.

B.1.   Facing down and standing improper (i.e. man in girl's place) the first man, with arm round partner's waist, promenades her down the middle, swings her half way round (counter-clockwise) and promenades her back. Cast one place (progression).

B.2.   Right and left through, i.e. cross right with partner: two men change places while two girls do the same: repeat both movements.

4. ALL THE WAY TO GALWAY

>   (Devised by Rich Castner. The dance is also known as "Paddy on the Turnpike.")

Music: "All the Way to Galway" or any other similar reel, such as "Farewell to Whisky" (CDM 4), played not too fast.

Form: Longways, duple improper. 1st couples have crossed sides.

A.1.   1st couple down the centre and separate left and right, returning outside to place.

A.2.   Everybody do-si-do partners, then contrary.

B.1.   Balance and swing contrary, finishing facing other line with girl on right.

B.2.   Half promenade, half right and left through.

THE BELFAST HORNPIPE

HUNT THE SQUIRREL

HULL'S VICTORY

ALL THE WAY TO GALWAY

PORTLAND FANCY

THE MANCHESTER OR RICKETT'S HORNPIPE

5. PORTLAND FANCY

Music: "Portland Fancy" or any similar jig.

Form: Progressive Double Longways or Double Sicilian Circle: Line of two couples facing line of two couples: man with partner on his right.

A. Circle eight once round.

B. Breaking the eight into two four-handed sets, opposite couples dance "Right and Left through" (i.e. cross right with opposite, men turn partners with left hand to change places, and repeat to original places).

C.1. The four handed sets then dance "Ladies' Chain" (i.e. two girls give right hands to each other and cross to opposite men, who turn them round with left hand, right hand on girls' waists. The girls cross back to partners, who turn them with left hand to places).

C.2. The lines of four meet, retire and pass through to meet next line of four approaching.

6. BUTTERFLY HORNPIPE (Warwickshire)
(Dance collected by Cecil Sharp-Country Dance Book 1)

Music: Manchester or Rickett's Hornpipe or any other hornpipe.

Form: Progressive Longways contra or Sicilian Circle (couple facing couple round the room).
(Warning 1st couples to make arch first).

A.1. Right hands across and back with the left.

A.2. Over and under arches (1 over 2, and 2 over 1: repeat).

B. (Once only.) Couples swing and change places.

7. WASHINGTON QUICK STEP

Music: "The Lady in the Boat" or any other suitable tune.

Form: Progressive Longways: man facing girl (four handed sets).

A.1. Right hands across and back.

A.2. First man leads partner down the middle, arm on her waist, turns half way round (counter-clockwise) and leads back again to cast a place round second couple, who move up (progression). The first couple are now improper.

B.1. "Ladies' Chain."

B.2. Partners advance, retire and swing: men and girls finishing up on own side.

8. GALOPEDE

(Collected by Cecil Sharp – Country Dance Book 1 – and included by permission of Messrs. Novello & Co.)

Music: "Galopede" or any other rant tune.

Form: Longways set for four, five, or six couples: man facing girl.

A.1. The men and girls advance (with double step), retire, and cross over by the right, turning right to occupy the opposite place.

A.2. As A.1.

Repeat to places.

B. All swing partners.

C. First couple swing from top to bottom of set while other couples clap and move up.

Repeat the whole figure until the original top couple are back in place.

9. WINSTER GALOP (a variant of above)

(As danced by the Morris dancers in Winster, Derbyshire, where the team consists entirely of men, half of whom dance on the women's side.)

Music: "Winster Galop".

Form: As in "Galopede".

A.1. As in "Galopede". When the dancers cross over to change places they break into an easy walk as they turn to face. Otherwise double step.

A.2. As A.1.

B.1. The top couple, followed by the others, cast off left and move round up the middle to places. As each couple reaches the top place, each man offers right arm to partner, and they dance the cast round, arm in arm, with a step-hop.

B.2. The top couple (girl holding the man's shoulders) swing down to the bottom, while other dancers clap. (Double step.)

Repeat until the last couple dance down the middle, then play B music once more, during which all swing partners in position.

THE LADY IN THE BOAT

GALOPEDE

WINSTER GALOP

BONNY BREAST KNOT (Sussex)

THE WHITE COCKADE

10. **BONNY BREAST KNOT (Sussex Version)**

    (Collected by Mary Neal and Clive Carey at Knapp, West Sussex, and first published in the "Esperance Morris Book". Republished by permission.)

Music: "Bonny Breast Knot."

Form: Longways, duple minor. Short sets of 4 or 5 couples recommended.

A.1.   1st girl dances a figure eight round 2nd couple, while 1st man dances completely round them clockwise. (Polka step.) He optionally right-hands his partner into the figure.

A.2.   1st man figure eight while 1st girl dances round counter-clockwise. Optional left hand pass to begin.

B.1.   1st man leads partner down and back to place. It is suggested that 2nd couple follows as in "Corn Rigs" and makes an arch for the 1st couple, all polkaing home in bars 5–8.

B.2.   Couples swing round each other 1½ times; crossed hands or ballroom hold.

11. **YORKSHIRE SQUARE EIGHT**

    (From Three More Dances of the Yorkshire Dales and included by permission of Miss L. M. Douglas.)

Music: "The White Cockade" or any other suitable tune.

Form: A square set for four couples numbered round counter-clockwise.

A.1.   First and third couples advance and retire, then change places, dancing polka step with ball-room hold and moving in ball-room direction.

A.2.   Second and fourth couples the same.

B.1.   First and third couples repeat and return to places.

B.2.   Second and fourth couples the same.

A.3.   First and second couples right and left hands across. Third and fourth couples the same.

A.4.   "Ladies' Chain" in each four.

B.3.   First and fourth couples right and left hands across.
Third and second couples the same.

B.4.   "Ladies' Chain" in each four.

A.5.   Girls to centre and out. While the girls come out, the men go in and then turn and swing the girl on their left.

A.6.   Men promenade new partner to places.

B.5 etc.   Repeat this figure (girls to centre, etc.) three times until all are in original places.

12. NORFOLK LONG DANCE

Music: "The Perfect Cure" or any other suitable tune.
              (This tune was collected from Mr. Herbert Mallet, of Norfolk.)

Form: Progressive Longways: man facing girl (four handed sets).

A.1.   First and second couples, right and left hands across.

A.2.   Men and girls advance and retire twice. First time the girls pass inside the two men—the second time the men are inside.

B.1.   First couple lead down and back to places.

B.2.   Couples swing and change places (ball-room direction). The girls' hands on partners' shoulders; men's hands on girls' waists.

13. SPEED THE PLOUGH (Surrey)

(Collected by Cecil Sharp—Country Dance Book 1)

Music: "Speed the Plough" or any hornpipe.

Form: Progressive Longways contra: man facing partner (hands four).

A.1.   First couple visit the second girl, honour and retire. Then the same to her partner.

A.2.   First couple down the centre and back to places.

B.1.   All cross and turn right and cross back and turn left.   (Figure 8.)
              Girls passing above partner each time.

B.2.   Couples swing and change.

THE PERFECT CURE

SPEED THE PLOUGH

BONNY BREAST KNOT (Somerset and Devon)

BONNETS SO BLUE

14. BONNY BREAST KNOT (Somerset and Devon)

> (Collected by Maud Karpeles-Country Dance Book 1-and included by kind permission.)

Music: "Bonny Breast Knot" or any other suitable reel.

Form: Longways for as many as will: man facing girl.

　　　　　　 Triple minor set but can be danced as a set dance.

A.1.&2.   First man leads partner between the two girls, cast off and lead between the men, cast off and stand-first man between third couple and first girl between second couple, the two lines facing and taking hands.

B.   Balance four times (stepping first on to the left foot) and then first couple move into the middle place in the set (the line of men facing the line of girls). Repeat balance.

A.1.&2.   First couple arm right and pass at once to right hand corner to arm left. Arm right with own partner again and arm left with left hand corner.

B.   First couple lead down and back to the middle place, and everyone swing partners. If danced as a set dance the first couple remain in the bottom place after leading down.

15. BONNETS SO BLUE

> (Collected from William Kimber of Headington.)

Music: The same or any other jig.

Form: Progressive Longways contra: man facing partner (hands four).

A.   Right hands across and left hands across.

B.   First couple down centre and back into 2nd's place (galop sideways).

C.   Couples swing around each other.

16. DOUBLE LEAD THROUGH

(Collected from William Kimber of Headington.)

Music: Double Lead Through.

Form: Progressive Longways contra: man facing partner (hands four).

A.   Forward and back twice, bowing.

B.   First couple lead down and back. Second couple lead up and back.

C.1.   Polka stepping in position.

C.2.   Couples swing and change places.

17. CIRCLE WALTZ

Music: Any 32-bar length, such as "Bonny Tyneside" or "Star of the County Down".

Form: Either in Big Set for a large number of couples in one circle or concentric circles, or in small sets–of 5 couples, say, 5 times through for good length, or of 4 couples if no exchange of partners seems desirable.

A.   Taking hands, balance in, out. Each man helps his left-hand girl to waltz across to his right, as in Waltz Country Dance. All this 4 times.

B.   Keep the girl you've got. Take inside or both hands; sway in and out. Dropping hands, spin inwards to face. Repeat, swaying out and in, etc. Ballroom hold: 2 chassays in, 2 out, waltz a little way round the circle and start again.

DOUBLE LEAD THROUGH

THE STAR OF THE COUNTY DOWN

(Arrangement reprinted by permission of Boosey & Hawkes Music Publishers Ltd.)

18.   THE BIG SET — ALLEMANDE

Music: Any Reel or Jig. The music provides the rhythm only and no attempt is made to fit the figures to phrases or part phrases of the tune.

Form: A double circle of any size: men stand backs to centre, facing girls, who form the outer circle. Progressive.

The figures are "called" throughout and the Caller rings the changes on the following:

Figures and Calls: Honour partner, or Honour *new* partner.

Allemande Right (partners turn once round with right hands).

Allemande Left.

Back to Back Right (passing forward by right shoulder and back by left).

Back to Back Left.

Swing partners (with walking step or pivot).

Leave that girl and pass next door, *or*

Leave that girl and pass on two (or three, or four, or more places).

(Note that the girls remain in their original positions while the men move on to their left, i.e. Ball-room direction.)

All promenade (Ball-room direction).

All turn back (reverse direction).

The dance can be used as a "Paul Jones" in conjunction with other dances, the Caller stopping the music at any point in the dance.

3

Eighteen Traditional Dances collected by Peter Kennedy, together with "Princess Margaret's Fancy," devised by him.

Introduction

Edited by
Peter Kennedy

THE eighteen dances in this volume, which have been contributed by Peter Kennedy, are examples of the social dance forms surviving in the English villages. In editing and describing them, he has been forced, for the sake of simplicity, to standardize material which is essentially fluid and changeable. Dance versions differ from village to village : the sequence of movements may change overnight and an unintentional variation may become the established local practice.

The production of a text book of folk material inevitably tends to stereotype performance, but I hope that all those who use this one will be brave enough to interpret the notations liberally. Where there is so much local tolerance of form and style, he is bold indeed who would say " that is right " and " that is wrong."

With many of the current square and community dances it is necessary for the M.C. or Caller to decide just what version he will use for the occasion, and to inform the company accordingly. This fluidity may be irritating to those who like the unchanging stability of set figures to set music, but it is essential to the natural evolution of all living folk forms, and whatever is printed here will be disregarded in those communities where these dances are traditional. We who are not fortunate enough to live in such communities are glad to borrow the dances that they have evolved.

DOUGLAS KENNEDY.

1. THE TEMPEST (Wiltshire version)

This dance must at one time have been popular all over England, although its character, like " La Russe," is of the more recent Quadrille period. There are a number of versions: this one was collected at Seend in Wiltshire.

Music : Although a version of the " La Tempete " tune was collected at Seend, the particular version given here is one played by shepherds near Powburn, Northumberland.

Form : Progressive Quadrille. Four couples in a set. Two couples facing two couples in sets down the length of the room, the lines of four being arranged across the room. On reaching either end, the fours " remain neutral " for one turn of the dance. They then turn round and partners exchange places: those who have been "Outsides" become "Insides" and vice versa.

A. CIRCLE EIGHT. Join hands and circle left : then circle back to places (" Rant " or double-step).

B. Couples take ballroom hold and galop across (men passing back to back). Galop back to places (girls passing back to back). Repeat galop.

C. INSIDES STAR : OUTSIDES SWING. Centre four form right hands across while Outsides (contraries) balance to each other four times. Insides left hands across while Outsides swing.

D. FORWARD, BACK, CLAP AND PASS ON. Join hands in lines of four, dance forward and back. Clap hands in position and pass through to meet the opposite line in the next set. (Those with their backs to the music make arches.)

2. THE RIFLEMAN

Collected Weardale, Co. Durham from Miss Cole who first danced it at Alston in Cumberland where it was known as " The Galopade ".

Music : " Galopede " or any other similar polka tune. " Come Dance and Sing " is given here.

Form : Whole set longways in special formation. Any even number of couples in a set. Two lines of couples facing couples: men with girls on their right.

Steps : The " Rant " or double-step is used throughout.

A.1. MEET AND CROSS. All join hands in two lines : advance and retire. Forward again, dancers release hands, and, taking the contrary dancer with both hands, each man promenades his new partner in a small circle (ballroom direction) back into his place.

A.2. REPEAT TO PLACES.

B.1. LADIES CHAIN. All couples perform Ladies Chain—"Quadrille Style" —with the contrary. Girls give right hands and cross to the contrary men, who take them with left hand and pass them round behind under the left arm. Repeat to places.

B.2. TOPS DOWN THE MIDDLE. The two top couples take ballroom hold and dance to the bottom of the set while the other couples clap, moving up two places.

THE TEMPEST

COME DANCE AND SING

KA-FOO-ZALUM

CASTLES IN THE AIR

RUSSIAN CAVALRY

3. DROPS OF BRANDY (English version of " Strip the Willow ")

Music :   This dance takes its name from a tune in nine-eight time not now used for the dance. "Ka-foo-zalum" is given here, but any other similar Schottisches tune may be used. *Note :* No particular strain of music is connected with any particular part of the dance.

Form :   Longways Whole Set Dance.   Four or five couples in a set.

Steps :   A step-hop (Highland Schottische step) is used throughout.

THE SINGLE REEL FIGURE. (Using short arm grip throughout, first couple swing once and a half with right arm. First girl then goes down set to each man and swings once with left arm and back to partner with right. First man remains in centre of set while partner swings other men. On reaching bottom, he comes up set swinging partner with right and each other girl with left, until top of set is regained.

THE DOUBLE REEL FIGURE. First couple now swing down lines simultaneously. Meanwhile the next couple begins.

4. THE KIELDER SCHOTTISCHE (A " Three Reel ")

From Kielder, Northumberland. Only two figures performed traditionally but any other three-hand reel figures may be used in place of Double Arching.

Music :   " Castles in the Air " or any other tune in Highland Schottische time.

Form :   Man linked with two girls (or a girl with two men), as danced at Kielder by handkerchiefs or ribbons. Trios stand facing the music or in a circle round the room.

Bars 1-4.   STEPPING. Stepping in position. All three dancers facing front, using the Highland Schottische : " step " (right twice) forward 3 steps, " step " (left twice) backward 3 steps.

Bars 5-8.   DOUBLE ARCHING. Without releasing hands, handkerchiefs or ribbons, man raises right hand to make an arch and passes left hand girl under. She turns to right, back to place, and he follows under his own arch. Repeat with left hand arch and right hand girl.

(*NOTE : This dance may be used as a processional, the dancers moving forward twice in the First Part.*)

5. THE RUSSIAN BALLET (Progressive " Three Reel ")

Versions of this have been found in various parts of the country.

Music :   All kinds of march-time tunes in 2/4 or 6/8 are used. " The Russian Cavalry March " is given here.

Form :   Trios in circle round room facing ballroom direction, one behind the other. The centre man (or girl) moves one place forward at each new turn of the dance.

Steps :   Walk, with occasional double-step.

VERSION ONE (TWO-PART) :—1. Forward and back twice (3 steps each way) ; 2. Double arching as in Kielder Schottische. The above is repeated and each time the centre dancers move forward to pick up next two.

VERSION TWO (FOUR-PART) :—1. Forward (7 steps). Balance in position to right hand then left hand dancer ; 2. Reel of three (or hey) starting right shoulders with right hand dancer ; 3. Double arching ; 4. All perform four high-kicking balance steps, starting by swinging right leg up to the left. Centre dancer bows to right hand and bows to left hand dancer and moves on to next pair.

6. THE RING DANCE (Dorset)

As danced at Burton Bradstock, South Dorset. It was used as a " bringing-in " dance, starting with a small ring in the centre.

Music : Any reel tune of 32 bars. " Gilderoy " and " Dorsetshire Hornpipe " are given here.

Form : Grand Circle, all facing centre. Men with partners on their right.

Steps : " Rant "—double-step throughout.

A.1. Circle left.

A.2. Circle right.

B.1. Promenade partners.

B.2. Polka round with partner.

(*In the Dorset villages they keep the same partner throughout. The dance can be used progressively, the man keeping the left hand of his corner partner at the end of Circle Right, and promenading with her as his new partner.*)

7. THE DURHAM REEL (Durham Rangers)

The Durham Reel was first collected by Miss Violet Orde from Mrs. Shafto, a member of an old Durham family, and first published by the Society in " Five Popular Country Dances." Other versions were found in Goathland, North Yorkshire, and Edmundbyers in Durham. In these villages the tune Durham Rangers was associated with the local " Six Reel ".

Music : Miss H. Shafto, when recently visited said she thought " The White Cockade " was generally used for the dance in Durham. " Durham Rangers " is given here.

Form : Longways Whole Set Dance for six to eight couples, men facing girls.

Steps : " Rant " or double-step.

A. CIRCLE. From column formation, before starting join hands in a ring. Circle left (for 8 bars), and circle right. (Total: 16 bars.)

B. SINGLE CAST. All release hands and return to column formation, facing up. Men cast round to left and girls to right and return up centre to places. Repeat. (The repeat cast may be danced in the reverse direction, facing down.) (16 bars.)

A. DOUBLE CAST (or COACH AND HORSES). Partners cross hands behind back and cast round to left : return up centre to places. Repeat. (May be repeated in reverse direction ; the dancers—without releasing hands— turning outwards to change their direction.) (16 bars.)

B. THREAD THE NEEDLE. Join hands in a ring again, leaving gap between 1st man and partner. He leads the circle under an arch (made by the 1st and 2nd girls) to places. Repeat with 1st girl leading under arch made by 1st and 2nd men. (16 bars.)

A1.B1. Finish with a final Circle. (16 bars.)

GILDEROY

THE DORSETSHIRE HORNPIPE

DURHAM RANGERS

WHEN DAYLIGHT SHINES (Three meet)

THE HULLICHAN JIG

8. THREE MEET

This dance is called " The Six Reel " in some parts of Cumberland.

Music : Any 32 bars of jig (or reel) time. " When Daylight Shines " is given here.

Form : A threesome, man with two partners, facing another trio in a grand circle round the room (or in lines up and down the room). In one Gloucestershire version a Circle Six is used instead of the Elbow Swing figure. Although not generally danced progressively in the villages, the last figure can, however, be used for the trios to change places into the next set.

A.1. ADVANCE, RETIRE AND CROSS OVER. Man links arms with both his partners and they dance forward to meet the other trio with three steps. Retire to places. Then, without letting go arms, both trios cross to opposite places by promenading round each other, face-to-face and in ballroom direction.

A.2. REPEAT TO PLACES.

B.1. ELBOW SWING PARTNERS (OR CIRCLE SIX). Man hooks right elbow with right hand partners and swings twice round. Then left elbow with left hand partner. (OR Join hands in a ring of six and circle to left and back to right.)

B.2. SWING THREE. All " couple up " in trios to form a " basket " and pivot round on the spot. Alternatively trios may exchange positions, ballroom direction, while swinging (progression).

9. THE HULLICHAN

Music : " The Hullichan Jig " given here but other jig tunes may be used.

Form : Two couples in a line of four as for " The Four Hand Reel " with the girls back to back facing their partners.

Steps : When dancing in position vigorous jig steps are employed. One favourite step is the " skip-back-step." For the swing a pivot step is used, standing shoulder to shoulder (right), and clasping partner's hands behind backs.

A.1. STEPPING. After honouring partners, the girls turn round and step to each other. (8 bars.)

A.2. SWING. (8 bars.) After swinging the girls finish facing contrary partners.

B.1. B.2. Balance to contraries and swing. (16 bars.)

A.1. A.2. The men the same. (16 bars.)

B.1. B.2. Balance to partners and swing.

REPEAT TO PLACES.

HULLICHAN ROUNDABOUT

Form : *Grand circle, men with partners on right, all facing centre as for 2nd figure of " Circassian Circle."*

Stepping, and Swing partners as for "The Hullichan." (16 bars.)

Finish facing next partner and repeat as many times as required (progressing, men clockwise and girls counter-clockwise).

10. THE PROGRESSIVE SIX REEL

Music : " Knick Knack " given here but any 32 bars of reel (or jig) tune may be used.

Form : Man (or girl) with two partners facing another three in circle round (or line up and down) the room.

A.1. SIX HAND STAR. Right hands and left hands across. " Rant " or double-step.

A.2. REEL OF THREE. Man (or girl) faces right hand partner, and, working in threes, without giving hands, all perform a hey or figure of eight.

B. DOUBLE ARCHING. Centre dancer joins hands with both partners, raises right hand and passes left hand dancer below. Then goes under himself (or herself). Raise left hand and pass right hand dancer below, etc.

C. FORWARD, BACK, CLAP AND PASS ON. The " threes " move forward and back with three walk-steps, clap, and pass through to meet the next three. Those facing ballroom direction may make arches over the opposite trio.

11. THE TWELVE REEL

Music : Any Reel or Jig played twice through. "Russian Cavalry" on p. 38 is suggested for this dance.

Form : Four men, each with two partners, standing in a small square.

MEET AND TRADE

A.1. Head men link arms and the two " trios " advance and retire. Advance again and the contrary girls change places with each other and fall back with the contrary man. (8 bars).

A.2. Side " trios " do this. (8 bars).

B. REPEAT TO PLACES. (16 bars).

C.1. DANCE ROUND. Head men take right hand partners and, with waltz hold, dance round inside, ballroom direction. (4 bars) Repeat with left hand partners. (8 bars).

C.2. Side men do this. (8 bars).

D.1. BASKET SWING. All " trios " form baskets and swing in position. (8 bars).

D.2. CIRCLE. Join hands 12 and circle left all the way round to places. (8 bars).

12. THE TRIUMPH (or Follow Your Lovers)

Music : " The Triumph " or any similar tune.

Form : Progressive Longways Dance (Duple set).

Steps : In Northumberland, where this version was collected, the dancers use " Rant " or double-step throughout.

A. LEAD DOWN AND BACK (or HANDS ACROSS). 1st couple lead down the centre and back (2nd couple may follow as in Corn Rigs—see No. 13). Return to places. OR right and left hand star. (8 bars).

B. FOLLOW YOUR LOVERS. 2nd man gives left hand to 1st girl and leads her down the centre. Her partner follows (also down the centre) and draws up level on the far side of his partner so that she is between the two men. The 2nd man turns the 1st girl round and, to return up the centre, gives his right hand to the 1st man's left to make an arch behind her head. He keeps left hand holding girl's left and 1st man holds her right with his right hand. They return " in triumph " to places. (8 bars).

C. DANCE ROUND. Both couples dance round each other, ballroom direction (ballroom or cross hands hold. (8 bars).

KNICK-KNACK

THE TRIUMPH (or Follow your lovers)

CORN RIGS

BARBARY BELL

HEXHAM RACES

13. CORN RIGS

Music : " Corn Rigs " and any other similar tunes. (Hornpipes such as " The Breakdown," " Staten Island," " Durham Rangers," etc., played fairly fast. See The Fiddler's Tune Book.)

Form : Progressive Longways (Duple set) 4-5 couples in a set.

Step : " Rant " or double-step is used throughout (except for the lead down).

A.1. ROUND THE OUTSIDE. The 1st girl turns to her right and dances round the 2nd girl and 2nd man to her partner's place. At the same time the 1st man follows her round the 2nd girl but returns up centre to his partner's place. All step in position facing partners.

A.2. This figure is repeated to places, the 1st man leading.

B.1. DOWN THE CENTRE. The 1st couple lead down (single-step), followed by the 2nd couple, who make an arch for the 1st couple to pass under. Both return to places (double-step).

B.2. DANCE ROUND. Both couples dance round each other, ballroom direction (progression).

14. BARBARY BELL

Music : " Barbary Bell " (St. Patrick's Day), and " The American Dwarf " or any other jigs are suitable.

Form : Progressive Longways (Duple Set). 4-5 couples in a set.

A.1. DOUBLE CHANGE SIDES. The two girls and two men advance and retire. Cross over (the girls passing under an arch made by the men).

A.2. REPEAT TO PLACES (the girls making an arch for the men). (*In the villages this is performed in a more elaborate manner: The two girls and two men keep right hands joined throughout. After crossing over, 1st and 2nd girls and 1st and 2nd men change places—the 1st man and 1st girl passing under his or her own arch.*)

B.1. DOWN THE CENTRE. 1st couples lead down the centre and back to places.

B.2. DANCE ROUND. Both couples dance round each other with two-step, ballroom direction (progression).

15. PINS AND NEEDLES

The name of this dance is believed to be a corruption of " Prince of Wales," a dance air. This version was collected in Northumberland.

Music : " Hexham Races " or any other jigs.

Form : Progressive Longways (Duple Set). 4-5 couples in a set.

A.1. BALANCE FOUR IN LINE. 1st couples give right hands and turn half round to stand between 2nd couples, to whom they give left hands. Keeping hands, balance twice in line of four. Turn contrary partner half round with left hand. Balance four in line again.

A.2. Turn contraries half around again so that 1st couples are again in centre. Balance in line again. 1st couples then turn half around and balance to each other in the centre of the set.

B.1. DOWN THE CENTRE. 1st couples lead down the centre of the set. They return up centre to 2nd couples' places (progression).

B.2. DANCE ROUND. Both couples take ballroom hold and dance once around each other.

16. PRINCESS MARGARET'S FANCY (Peter Kennedy 1949)

Music : The selected quadrille tune or any other (played 10 times).

Form : Quadrille Set of four couples.

This dance contains many of the characteristic movements which occur in the traditional dances collected by Peter Kennedy in various country districts.

Introduction and Finale

A. SPANISH WALTZ FIGURE. All join hands in a ring of eight. Balance one step to centre and back. Men put corner partners, on their left, into partner's place, on the right. (4 bars). Repeat until partners are regained. (12 bars).

B. HEEL AND TOE (*Two-step promenade*). Partners join hands and face ballroom direction. Starting with outside foot, place heel on ground in front then toe to the rear. Walk forward four steps. Take ballroom hold and two-step " waltz " to halfway positions. (8 bars). Repeat to places. (8 bars).

Figure

A.1. LEADING COUPLE DANCE SOLO. Leading couple only perform solo figure while others clap. They can two-step " waltz " round inside the set, swing in position, promenade, or (keeping inside hand) girl can dance twice round her partner etc. etc. (8 bars).

A.2. OVER THE TOP. Leading couple, with inside hands, make an arch and pass it over the heads of the other dancers (ballroom direction, man inside, girl outside set). Men kneel, girls curtsey and clap. (8 bars.)

B. STRIP THE WILLOW. Leading couple hook right elbow or use short arm grasp and turn each other once. The girl goes to the 2nd man and turns with the left, and then returns to partner with the right. This is repeated with 3rd and 4th men. Leading couple continue turning to end of music. (16 bars).

Break or Chorus Figure

C.1. LADIES MILLWHEEL, GENTS ON THE OUTSIDE TRACK. All four girls go to the centre and facing clockwise move round slowly with right hand on right shoulder of girl in front, using a short balance step. At the same time the men move round the outside in the opposite direction. (8 bars).

C.2. GENTS MILLWHEEL, LADIES OUTSIDE. On meeting partner after moving once round circle all hook left elbow with partners and exchange places. men millwheel slowly round to the centre clockwise while girls dance round the outside—ballroom direction. (8 bars).

D. SASHAY AND TWIRL PARTNERS. All return to places and take ballroom hold with partners. Sashay (sidestep) twice towards the centre, then men twirl partners once under left arm. " Waltz " partners back to places with one revolution. (8 bars). Repeat this. (8 bars).

FIGURE is repeated for each couple in turn followed by the BREAK. Then finish with the INTRODUCTION.

PRINCESS MARGARET'S FANCY

NINEPINS (OATS, PEAS, BEANS)

17. NINEPINS (QUADRILLE)

Music : At least 48 bars of reel or jig tune. The music stops suddenly when the four men (or girls) and the " Ninepin " are circling in the centre.

Form : Quadrille set of four couples with an extra man or girl in the centre as the " Ninepin."

A.1. HEADS GALOP. 1st and 3rd couples take ballroom hold, and, keeping to right, galop to each other's places. Turn round and galop back to places and turn round again. (The " Ninepin " in the centre must dodge them.)

A.2. SIDES GALOP.

B.1. HEADS CIRCLE FOUR. 1st and 3rd couples take hands four round the " Ninepin " and circle left and right. The " Ninepin " steps in the centre, turning to right and left.

B.2. SIDES CIRCLE FOUR.

" NINEPIN " SWINGS EACH GIRL. All couples start by swinging partners but men go to the centre as the " Ninepin " takes their partners. " Ninepin " goes to 1st girl and swings while her partner moves to centre and steps. " Ninepin " leaves 1st girl (who stands) and goes to 2nd girl, while her partner swings with 1st man in centre. " Ninepin " goes to 3rd girl while the three men circle. " Ninepin " goes to 4th girl while the four men circle. " Ninepin " then joins the circle, making five, until the music stops suddenly : all the men (and " Ninepin ") rush to partner the four girls. The odd man out becomes " Ninepin " next time.

ANOTHER VERSION (Northumberland).

A.1. Eight hands round to left (4 bars) and right (4 bars) back to places.

A.2. Grand chain halfway and promenade home.

B.1. Balance to corners (4 bars).
Here the " Ninepin " intercepts and steals one girl.
Swing partners (New " Ninepin " goes to centre).

B.2. Promenade round.

18. THE PIN REEL

Form : A Grand Circle, all facing centre, with extra men (or girls) in the centre as " Pins."

A.1. Join hands, advance and retire to centre and back, and circle left.

A.2. Advance and retire again, and circle right.
(During 1 and 2, " Pins " form a basket in the centre.)

B.1. Grand chain, starting by giving right hand to partner. The " Pins " join in this movement. When the music stops take the nearest partner.

B.2. Waltz, polka, schottische, etc. Those left out become the new " Pins " and go to the centre of the ring.

4

The notation of twenty CONTRA DANCES, with The Double Quadrille (Double Sicilian Circle), and seventeen tunes.

Introduction

Edited by
Douglas Kennedy

THE Longways Country Dance has been in vogue for more than three hundred years. Derived from the ritual processions and rounds of country custom, it has not only survived in the villages but has had an independent and quite important career among the social dance forms of fashionable folk in Europe and in America. To England has been given the chief credit for its development and export abroad. Our ancestors took it across the Atlantic and many examples of the longways contra dance have survived in Canada and in the United States, alongside the Round and Square Dances. Overseas the longways dances are invariably called Contra Dances, emphasizing the fact that each dancer stands opposite to his partner.

The contra dances printed in this selection are simple arrangements of 4-handed (or quadrille) figures, including a progression of one place up or down the set. Normally in the contra dances the men stand on one side with their partners opposite them and the set is divided into smaller units which consist of two couples or three couples—according to the figures to be performed. In many of the dances the first man and first woman change places and stand on the " wrong " side of the set, keeping those relative positions until they reach the bottom of the set, when they change back to their proper sides. Such dances are conveniently called " improper." When the long sets are divided up into two couple (or 4-handed) units, these minor units are called " duple." When the small units consist of three couple (or 6-handed) units, they are called " triple." In both duple and triple dances the first or leading couple moves down one place on each progression, the second couples all moving up a place. In a triple dance the second and third couples, as they work up the set, keep changing their numbers (but not their positions relative to each other) with each progression. For this reason the triple dances are more difficult to perform and are confusing at first for the second and third couples. For the first couples, who remain a leading couple until they reach the bottom of the set, there is not the same difficulty.

It has been presumed that the reader of this book already understands the meaning of such terms as " ladies' chain," " right and left through," " lead down and cast," " do-si-do," " half promenade," " contrary partner," etc.

The music for these contra dances can be almost any traditional air in reel or jig time. These folk dance tunes are normally in two parts, and each part is repeated. That is to say, they are played A A, B B. Where the dance requires more music than is provided by this formula, an additional unit can be obtained by playing an extra A B. Only occasionally does one find a suitable tune providing an A, B, C. In some dances the association of a particular air is indicated by the name of the dance, and in certain cases versions of these named airs are printed in this book. In other cases the name of the dance is now just a label which may have been derived from a one-time association with a particular tune but that association, always loose in the progressive country dances, has since been lost. For this reason some of the dances are known by several names but to avoid confusion not more than two names have been given here to any one dance. Certain tunes have been suggested but these are only recommendations and many other reels and jigs may be equally suitable.

I cordially acknowledge my indebtedness to Al Brundage and Ralph Page of the U.S.A. for their permission to use their printed descriptions as my source for certain dances. My thanks are also due to Patrick Shuldham-Shaw for helping to choose tunes and for suggesting harmonies.

DOUGLAS KENNEDY.

DUPLE PROPER

1. JAKIE'S HORNPIPE or MISS McLEOD'S REEL

A.1.   1st couple down the centre (man's arm round partner's waist), turn half round as a couple and lead back up the centre (girl on man's side, man on girl's side) and cast round 2nd couple, who move up (progression). The 1st couple is now improper.

A.2.   Ladies' chain.

B.1.   1st and 2nd couples whole promenade round each other.

B.2.   Forward and back and partners swing, men and girls finishing up on own side.

2. PRINCESS ROYAL

A.1.   1st and 2nd couples right hands across and back.

B.1.   All lead down in couples, turn and lead back.   1st couple cast round 2nd couple who move up into 1st couple's place (progression).

B.2.   Partners balance and swing.

3. ROAD TO CALIFORNIA

(Suggested tune : " Mason's Apron ")

A.1.   1st man and 1st girl cross over the set to the place below and face out ; all join hands down each line and dancers balance.   All turn with right hand once round and balance in line again.

A.2.   All turn with left hand once round and then 1st couple meet in the centre of the set and swing.

B.1.   1st couple down the centre, back and cast round second couple who move up (progression).

B.2.   Right and left through.

4. ARKANSAS TRAVELLER

A.1.   The two lines of dancers each join hands, lead forward, back and cross right over, and, releasing hands, turn round.

A.2.   Repeat forward and back and cross back to places.

B.1.   Right hands across and back.

B.2.   1st couples swing in the centre.

A.3.   1st couples lead down the centre and turn as a couple (clockwise) : come back home and cast (progression).

B.3.   Right and left through.

MISS McLEOD'S REEL

MASON'S APRON

ARKANSAS TRAVELLER

MAGGIE BROWN'S FAVORITE

FAREWELL TO WHISKY

LADY WALPOLE'S REEL

5. CAMP TOWN HORNPIPE

A.1. 1st couple down the outside and come back home.

A.2. 1st couple lead down the centre, turn as a couple (clockwise): come back home and cast off.

B.1. Ladies' chain.

B.2. Balance and swing your own.

DUPLE IMPROPER
(1st couples have crossed over; men on girl's side and girls on men's side)

6. HAYMAKERS JIG
(Suggested tune: "Maggie Brown's Favorite")

A.1. Balance and swing the one below.

A.2. 1st couple balance and swing partners and stand between 2nd couple.

B.1. Down the centre, four in line: turn toward contraries, lead back and cast (progression).

B.2. Ladies' chain.

7. TIMBER SALVAGE REEL
(Suggested tune: "Farewell to whisky")

A.1. Do-si-do with the one below (back to back); do-si-do with your own.

A.2. 1st couples balance and swing.

B.1. 1st couples down the middle, turn inwards lead back and cast (progression).

B.2. Right hands across and back.

8. SPEED THE PLOUGH (or LADY WALPOLE'S REEL)

A.1. Balance and swing the one below.

A.2. 1st couple down the centre, turn inwards, lead back and cast (progression).

B.1. Ladies' chain.

B.2. Half promenade and half right and left.

9. GREEN MOUNTAIN VOLUNTEER
(Suggested tune : " Doc Boyd's Jig ")

A.1.   Left hand file (men's side) balance and swing the one below, while right hand file (girl's side) promenade down the centre and back (down, with girl on right, back, girl on left).

A.2.   Same in reverse (i.e. right hand file balance and swing, etc.)

B.1.   1st couple down the centre, turn inwards, lead back and cast (progression).

B.2.   Right and left through.

10. PIPER'S FANCY
(Suggested tune : " The New Rigged Ship ")

A.1.   Left hand file balance and swing the one below; right hand file promenade down single file and back.

A.2.   Same in reverse.

B.1.   1st couple balance and swing.

B.2.   1st couple down the centre, lead back and cast (progression).

A.3.   Ladies' chain.

B.3.   Half promenade, half right and left.

11. THE MERRY DANCE
(Suggested tune : " The Blackberry Quadrille ")

A.1.   1st couple down the outside and back, taking the 2nd couple (girl on the man's right going down, on his left coming back). 2nd couple turn the 1st couple inward so that all four dancers are now facing down.

A.2.   Down the centre, four abreast, turn toward contraries, lead back and cast (progression).

B.1.   Ladies' chain.

B.2.   Half promenade and half right and left.

DOC BOYD'S JIG

THE NEW RIGGED SHIP

THE BLACKBERRY QUADRILLE

THE LADY OF THE LAKE

THE FAIRY DANCE (Fisher Laddie)

CROCKER'S REEL

12. THE LADY OF THE LAKE

A.1.   Balance and swing the one below.

A.2.   1st couple balance and swing your own.

B.1.   1st couple down the centre, turn inward, lead back and cast (progression).

B.2.   Ladies' chain.

13. MISS BROWN'S REEL or FAIRY DANCE

A.1.   1st girl swings 2nd man; 1st man swings second girl.

A.2.   1st couple down the centre, turn inward, lead back and cast (progression).

B.1.   Balance and swing partners.

B.2.   Right and left through.

TRIPLE PROPER
(sets working in units of 3 couples)

14. STEAMBOAT QUICKSTEP or SACKETT'S HARBOUR
(Suggested tune: "Crocker's Reel")

A.   Forward and back six; circle left (6 hands) three quarters' round.

B.   1st couple down the centre (the set is now *across* the room); lead back and cast (progression).

A.   Right elbow swing with partner, left elbow with corner (man faces down, girl up).   Repeat with partner (right elbow) and other corner (left elbow).

B.   Forward and back and circle right (6 hands), three quarters' round (bringing the set back to its normal position).

15. BEAUX OF ALBANY
(Suggested tune: "Spitfire Reel")

A.1. Top two couples balance and swing.

A.2. Top two couples follow each other down the centre. Each turns as a couple and comes back home. 1st couple cast (progression).

B.1. Right hands across and back (top two couples).

B.2. Bottom two couples right and left through.

16. CHORUS JIG

A. 1st couple down the outside, turn and come back home.

B. 1st couple down the centre, lead back and cast (progression).

C. Right elbow swing with partner, left with corner (the man faces down and the girl faces up). Repeat with partner and other corner.

D. 1st couple balance and swing in centre.

NOTE: With more experienced dancers, the set may be duple minor and all may dance simultaneously the right elbow swing (partner) and left elbow swing (with contrary).

17. FISHER'S HORNPIPE
(Suggested tune: "The Big Corral")

A.1. 1st couple down the outside.

A.2. 1st couple down the centre, turn inward, lead back and cast (progression).

B.1. Six-hand circle left and right.

B.2. The top two couples right and left through.

SPITFIRE REEL

CHORUS JIG

THE BIG CORRAL

MAJOR MACKIES JIG

DOUBLE QUADRILLE

TRIPLE IMPROPER
(1st couples have crossed over; men on girl's side and girls on men's side)

18. ST. PATRICK'S DAY IN THE MORNING

A.1. 1st couple down the outside, turn and come back home.

A.2. 1st couple down the centre, turn inward, lead back and cast (progression).

B.1. Forward six and back, circle six half way round (left).

B.2. Forward six and back once more and circle six (right) back to places.

C.1. 1st and 2nd couples right hand across and back.

C.2. 1st and 2nd couples ladies' chain.

19. LADY BOGART'S REEL
(Suggested tune: "Major Mackie's Jig")

A.1. 1st couples balance and swing.

A.2. 1st couples down the centre, turn inward, lead back and cast.

B.1. The lines of three dancers go forward six and back; middle dancer in each line (1st man and 1st girl) hold right hand high and left hand low and change the end dancers over.

B.2. 2nd and 3rd couples swing partners; 2nd and 3rd couples half right and left up and down the set. (2nd couple pass right only.)

20. BARRY'S BEST (Advanced)

A.1. All three couples forward and back and do-si-do. 1st couple separate and each dancer joins hands with the two immediately below; circle (hands three) to the left half way round until 1st man and 1st girl are on the outside of the set. 1st man and 1st girl then pop through an arch made by the two other dancers in the ring, to the middle place, and swing as a couple, while the other two dancers continue to turn round into their original places.

A.2. While the 1st couple swings, the outside couples dance right and left round them, back to places.

B.1. 1st couple down the centre, turn inward, lead back to original place and cast.

B.2. Ladies' chain.

DOUBLE SICILIAN CIRCLE

21. DOUBLE QUADRILLE. (Two couples standing side by side facing a similar line of four dancers, and the sets of eight disposed in a circle round the room).

A. Circle eight hands round to the left.
Come back again.

B.1. Outside four lead contrary down the middle and back. Inside four lead contrary up the middle and back.

B.2. Outside and inside fours dance right and left through, then circle left and circle right.

C. Partners dance round the opposite couple 2 or 3 times and a half then link up with the next door couple to face the new oncoming four.

5

Eighteen dances from various sources, including reels, threesomes, waltzes, mixers and contras, together with sixteen tunes.

Introduction

Edited by
Michael Bell

THE contents of this Manual have been garnered by Michael Bell from a variety of sources. Outstanding from the point of view of the preservation of the living tradition are the English reels from Dorset and Wiltshire and the Country Dances from Leicestershire and Westmorland. Several of these are " stepping " dances.

Certain of the dances are particularly useful for building varied programmes. These include the type, so popular on the other side of the Atlantic and known there as " mixers ", which allow the man to change his partner and extend his social and dance experience.

The additional dances in waltz time will be welcomed, for they provide a contrast to the jigs and polkas in which the English repertory is so rich. Equally welcome will be the three-somes for a man with two partners. There are more contra-dances to swell the contents of Community Dances Manual No. 4. These, with versions of the ever popular Sicilian Circle, some " devised " out of traditional material by present-day " callers ", complete the contents of this Manual.

Where the dances do not already possess their associated tunes, Mr. Bell has chosen melodies from among the ever-increasing corpus of traditional dance airs. He wishes to acknowledge his indebtedness to Nan Fleming-Williams for her assistance.

I hope that this collection will give particular pleasure to all those M.C.s who conduct Barn Dances and Square Dances. They will be able to select a version of a variable dance and feel the satisfaction of fitting it to the occasion. To these I would also offer a word of encouragement on the use of " prompt calls ", even in English country dances. The simple community dance forms lend themselves to a rapid visual presentation, especially if supplemented by a brief phase of well-timed calling. Some of the spontaneous character of the dance is lost if the treatment by the M.C. is too prosy and slow. Through prompting, as the dancers first feel their way into the figures and steps, they have the impression of discovering the dances for themselves.

Further, I would like to urge that the material in this and other Manuals is raw material for M.C.s and dancers to mould and devise to their own enchantment.

DOUGLAS KENNEDY.

Note: The following abbreviations are used in the text:—
        CDM 1, 2, 3, 4 — Community Dance Manual 1, 2, 3, 4
        FSFS   — Folk Songs From Somerset

TWO ENGLISH REELS

1. STOKE GOLDING COUNTRY DANCE

As noted by Miss Lambert of Stoke Golding, Leicestershire.

Music Any brisk continuous reel, gradually accelerating. " Keel Row ", " Fairy Dance " (CDM 4), " Mason's Apron ", etc.

Form Longset for 4 or 5 couples.

1st man swings bottom girl. Crossed hands advised.

Bottom man swings 1st girl.

1st couple strips the willow to the bottom. Start *right*.

1st man inside, 1st girl outside the set, he hands her up over the girls and down over the men

and into the swing with the new leading man to start Round Two.

This is traditionally danced unphrased, the length of swing, etc., being ad lib., but beginners may find it easier to do it first of all as a timed dance for 4 couples.

2. WILTSHIRE SIX-HAND REEL

First collected in West Lavington from Mrs. Holliday by Mrs. Gregson of Devizes, and further investigated by John Burgess and Ioan Jenkins.

Music The " Six-Handed Clap Dance ", a version of which is given opposite.

Form Longways for three couples.

A.1. The men dance-walk a reel of 3, while girls do the same. (No. 1 as usual starts by passing No. 2 right shoulder.)

A.2. As A.1. But this may be stepped instead of walked.

B.1. 3 right hand shakes with partner, 3 claps with yourself. Do all this twice more then change places with partner, passing right shoulder.

B.2. Step to partners.

Repeat the sequence from these opposite places, and so on ad lib. Optionally, finish with an extra B music for " everybody swing ".

MIXER

3. BLAYDON RACES MIXER

Devised by William Scott of Hexham.

Music " Blaydon Races ".

Form Big Set, any number of couples in a circle or concentric circles.

1-8 All into the centre and back, twice.

9-16 Ballroom hold: 2 chassays in, 2 out—and short dance round circle (*or* repeat chassays).

17-24 Promenade.

25-32 Men pass on to the girl in front, balance and swing her and put her on right for next round.

The words to sing during 17-32 are:—

> O my lads you should have seen us gangin',
> Passing the folks along the road just as they were stannin',
> There were lots of lads and lasses there, all with smilin' faces,
> Gangin' along the Scotswood road to see the Blaydon races.

KEEL ROW

WILTSHIRE SIX HAND REEL

BLAYDON RACES

4. THE THREE SEA CAPTAINS

Devised by Patrick Shuldham Shaw.

Music   The version of " Three Sea Captains " printed opposite.

Form   Lines of 4, each of 2 couples—which face alternately up and down, as for " Wiltshire Tempest ".

A.   Circle left all the way and back.

B.1-8   Middle four dancers basket, while end men swing opposite girls.

9-12   Inside hand to partner. Lines forward and back.

13-20   Each left-hand couple raising an arch, all Dip and Dive rather compactly round the eight to places. Then one more change to progress.

This dance is perhaps easier, though less exciting, if " forward and back " is omitted and all 9-20 used for Dip and Dive.

DANCES IN WALTZ TIME

5. BELGIAN WALTZ

Music   A 48-bar length. For instance, alternate two 16-bar tunes (see below) each played 3 times consecutively.

Form   Sicilian Circle.

1-16   2 hands to partner, sway towards other couple and back. Change places with opposite girl, both spinning as you go, letting girls have inside track. Right hand to partner, forward and back and change places with her.   **Twice**

17-32   Right hand to opposite, forward and back and change. 2 hands to opposite, sway and change as above.   **Twice**

33-48   Right hand star, turn out, 2 claps. Left hand star, no clap, waltz on.

6. OTHER WALTZ DANCES

Useful variations of the Waltz Country Dance (CDM 1) exist as follows:—

(1)   The usual Waltz Country Dance figures can be danced in Double Sicilian Circle, 2 couples facing 2 couples. In the " balance in, left lady over " the girls will be passed completely round the eight hand ring.

(2)   The so-called " American Waltz Country Dance " starts with the " balance in " figure and each man *changes place* with his left-hand girl as he transfers her to his right. Then stars and waltz on. Only 32 bars.

(3)   The " American Spanish Waltz " is similar. Give inside hand to partner and balance forward and back to opposite couple. Give two hands to opposite girl and lifting her gently over, change places with her. Keep her inside hand, forward and back to partner, etc. Stars and waltz on. 32 bars.

16-BAR WALTZ TUNES: Many useful sequences for the above dances may be built out of 16-bar song airs such as " As I Walked Through the Meadows ", " Hares on the Mountains " and " O, Sally My Dear " (all in FSFS), " Figgy Pudding " (at Christmas), American songs like " Bow Down Your Head and Cry ", and the tunes printed opposite which have been slightly adapted for dance purposes. Choose a key people can sing in, and they probably will.

THE THREE SEA CAPTAINS

STILL I LOVE HIM

YARMOUTH

MY ROSE IN JUNE

See "DORSET SONG BOOK"

BLOW THE MAN DOWN

NEW ENGLAND CONTRA DANCES

7. BOYS OF OAKHILL (Beaux of Oakhill)

Music Any 32-bar jig.

Form Longways, duple improper. First couples have crossed sides.

A.1. 1st man takes 2nd girl, 2nd man 1st girl, so that 1st couple are back to back, all four in line, thus: 2nd girl   1st man 1st girl   2nd man. All galop neighbour down and back.

A.2. Balance and swing the girl you've got, finishing facing other line with her on your right.

B.1. Ladies Chain.

B.2. Half Promenade, Half right and left through.

(Polkaing across in a Half Promenade has no American traditional backing.)

The very last time, optionally finish with " Lines advance and retire: swing your partners ", instead of B.2 or to an extra B.3. This traditional finish can be applied to any New England contra.

In the American *balance* use the *swing-over* style, with the man definitely more vigorous than his partner, not the English *set*.

8. LADIES TRIUMPH

Music No special reel or jig is necessary, but " Ladies Triumph " is recommended.

Form Longways, duple proper.

A.1. 2nd man takes 1st girl down the centre (not too far), her left hand in his left hand, 1st man pursuing immediately behind. Both bring her back in triumph, as in Warwicks version (CDM 3).

A.2. 1st man takes 2nd girl, 2nd man pursuing, etc.

B.1. 1st couple down the centre, (not too far), return and cast round 2nd couple who give a helping arm, as is usual in the American longways, never in the English.

B.2. Right and left through. Optional hand to partner, not to neighbour.

9. THE TEMPEST (Vermont version)

Collected by Maud Karpeles. (See " Twelve Traditional Country Dances ".)

Music " Ap Shenkin " or any other jig. " Kitty Magee " makes a good alternative.

Form Special double longways. *Ones* consist of two couples in line, facing down. *Twos* are two couples facing each other across the set.

A.1. Ones hand in hand down the centre and backwards* to place. For the rest of the sequence, the line of 4 divides, each One dancing with the nearest Two.

A.2. Circle 4, left and right. **B. 1-8** Ladies Chain. Let the men do the work!

B.9-16 Half promenade, half right and left through, and lead partner to progressed place— the Ones reforming one place down, Twos again facing one place up.

(*It is usual, in New England, for the first couples to turn around to return up the set—Ralph Page.)

LADIES TRIUMPH

AP SHENKIN (The Tempest)

10. THE GOOD GIRL

Music Any reel or jig.

Form Longways, duple improper. First couples have crossed sides.

A.1. Balance and swing contrary, finishing facing other line with girl on right.

A.2. Circle left and right.

B.1. All take partners down and back.

B.2. Right and left through. *Or* Ladies Chain.

The hold for " take partners down the centre " in any American contra may be (a) inside hands; (b) crossed hands; (c) man's arm round girl's waist, her hand on his shoulder. The choice is the man's, according to the flow of the figures or the whim of the moment.

11. THE PLOUGHBOY

A version of the " Beaux of Albany " (CDM 4), devised for 3 couples by Maurice Culpan.

Music " The Curly-Headed Ploughboy ". In last round only, play **A-A-B-A**.

Form Longways for three couples.

A.1. Top 2 couples balance and swing.

A.2. Same 2 couples, down the centre, turn as a couple and return. 1st couple separates and turns down into 2nd place while 2nd couple moves up into 1st place.

B.1. Same 2 couples, right and left hand star.

B.2. 1st man in middle place, changes with 3rd girl, 1st girl with 3rd man. These same dancers then circle left halfway. Finally, 1st couple cast into 3rd place, while 3rd couple move up.

Repeat from new places ad lib.

TWO DORSET COUNTRY DANCES

12. DORSET TRIUMPH

A realisation by Peter Swann and the Ashmore Group of Thomas Hardy's manuscript notation.

Music The version of the " Triumph " opposite. Choose the tempo with care—not too slow for easy movement nor so fast as to impair the dignity of the dance.

Form Longways for any number of couples.

Step Walking step predominating, except perhaps in the return in C.

A.1. 2nd man and 1st girl set right and left to each other, moving forward and return to places turning right about.

A.2. 1st man and 2nd girl the same.

B.1. 2nd man takes 1st girl down the centre, her right hand in his right hand, while 1st man casts out and walks down his side of the set.

B.2. 2nd man having passed 1st girl from his left side in front of him to his right side, men join inside hands and bring her back in triumph, her partner with his left hand turning her right about into place.

C. All the men lead partners down by the right hand, turn them under their arms and bring them back, 1st couple casting a place, 2nd couple carrying straight on up.

Hardy describes this dance in action in " Under the Greenwood Tree ".

KITTY McGEE

THE CURLY HEADED PLOUGHBOY

THE TRIUMPH (Dorset version)

13. DORSET FOUR-HAND REEL

Collected by Mr. F. Masters, Bridport.

Music The two tunes opposite are two of many variants used in Dorset.

Form 2 couples in line, thus: 1st man   1st girl 2nd girl   2nd man.

A.1, A.2. Reel of 4—begin passing by the right—to places. Repeat reel till almost home, men facing, thus: 2nd girl   2nd man   1st man   1st girl.

B.1. The men step to each other.

B.2. They turn to their partners who join in the stepping.

A.3, A.4. Repeat reel till home, leaving girls facing.

B.3. The girls step to each other.

B.4. They turn, etc. (B2).

Repeat ad lib.

It would be quite untraditional to attempt to standardise length of dance, type of stepping, use of hands, etc., but a useful length for community purposes is: twice through the above sequence, plus a " swing your partners ". In this case, warn the musicians, (traditionally melodeon and tambourine), to play each tune with its repeats twice and add an extra B. The A music may be walked or stepped. The stepping in the B musics can be any variant of the polka; a typical traditional bar of step would be:—tap right foot a little to left then a little to right of left foot, then close beside it and change (for repeat with other foot). Hands may be given in the A's either to feel one's way in reeling or to raise the temperature as the dance progresses.

SICILIAN CIRCLES

14. COTTAGERS

As collected by Mrs. Boyle in the Lake District before 1939 and recently investigated and recollected from Miss Short of Ambleside, by Ethyl Anderson.

Music Any jig, usually the " Quaker's Wife ".

Form Sicilian Circle.

A.1. Right and left hand star.

A.2. Set to partners with 2 chassay steps right and 2 left (8 beats). Swing partners with easy, not overstrenuous, pivot step (8 beats). Or Ladies Chain (" Rifleman " fashion).*

B.1. Basket twice round. All 4 advance together and men take initiative in placing arms round girls' backs, girls joining up behind men's backs. Withdraw in time for:—

B.2. Advance in couples and retire. Then dance past other couple to progress, with balance step as in " Pins and Needles ".

*Sometimes both these figures are used, making a 5-phrase sequence. Another version from South Westmorland gives stars, basket, Ladies Chain, advance and retire; the basket is quickly formed at the end of A.1. by the girls joining hands, then the men joining on top, the men lifting hands over, then the girls ditto, while the basket has already begun to move.

15. SICILIAN CIRCLES

These may be devised by the M.C. to suit the occasion, using rings, stars, baskets, corner crossings, hand turns, do-si-dos, swings, Ladies Chains, right and left throughs, etc.,—usually ending:—" forward and back and say good-bye, promenade on and hallo to the next." " Men pass shoulder to shoulder."

(1) An easy sequence for the inexperienced is as follows:—

A Circle left and right.

DORSET FOUR HAND REEL (First tune)

DORSET FOUR HAND REEL (Second tune)

B.1. " Duck for the oyster ".—Still holding hands, the couple which has the man inside ducks under and back, while the other couple moves over and back.
The other couple ducks under and back.
Then the first couple ducking right through, both couples move on.

B.2. Balance and swing partners.

(2) Besides being good mixers and excellent practice in prompt calling, these devised sequences can prepare the way for dances later in the session. For instance " The Tempest " (Vermont) can be led up to by calling in Sicilian Circle: " Circle left, circle right, ladies chain, half promenade, half right and left, forward and back and pass on."

(3) To " Haste to the Wedding "

A.1. Circle left and right.

A.2. Right hands across and back with the left.

B.1. Do-si-do contrary girl, 2 claps, and turns her with both hands, finishing facing partner.

B.2. Do-si-do partner, 2 claps, and each couple which has the man inside dives under other couple's arch, so progressing.

THREESOMES

For traditional North Country threesomes collected by Peter Kennedy, see CDM 3.

16. TRIPLE PROMENADE OR SILLY THREESOME

Devised by Kenneth and Sibyl Clark, taking a hint from the American " Eternal Triangle ".

Music   Any reel or jig.

Form   3 behind 3, each man with 2 partners, ballroom direction round the room. Spare men may hover in the centre till B.2, when they join in the tunnelling and compete for partners.

A.1.   Forward in threes.

A.2.   Arm right twice with right partner and left with left.

B.1.   As A.1.

B.2.   Girls form stationary arches for the men to tunnel under till, the music unexpectedly stopping, all form new lines of 3.

Repeat after minimum break.

In A.2 the M.C. may decide to call any other figure—reel of 3, basket, double arching, etc., —or, if the men have sufficient initiative, he may leave it to them to indicate their choice to the partners of the moment.

17. TEXAS PROGRESSIVE THREESOME

Music   " Lord Moira "   " The Staffordshire Hornpipe " or any similar tune.

Form   As in 16, but each man takes his partner's outside hand, girls joining inside hands behind him.

All start left foot, Step, close, step (1 bar).   Right foot, Step, close, step (1 bar). 4 walking steps.   Left heel, left toe, left, right, left,—here, the girls drop the inside hands and let the man turn them to face him.   Right heel, right toe, right, left, right,—here, the man moves forward, gently propelling the girls towards the man behind him.

18. THREESOME SICILIANS

These may be devised to suit any occasion when the sexes are unequal.   To the normal Sicilian Circle figures are now added the reel of 3, double arching, (CDM 3, p. 10), turn contra-corners (" Sacketts Harbour "), etc.

Useful, to any reel or jig, are:—

(1)   **Meeting Six** based on a sequence from Yorkshire.

A.1.   Threes take arms, forward and back, forward again and trade partners, opposite girls changing places and falling back with a new man.

A.2.   Repeat to places.

B.1.   Turn or arm right-hand partner with right, then left with left.

B.2.   Advance, retire and pass through, the threes who face ballroom direction making optional arches.

(2)   **Three Hand Star** devised by Nibs Matthews.

A.1.   Circle 6 left and right.

A.2.   Each man right-hand across with the 2 girls on his right. Then passing the other man by the left, he gives left hand across with the other girls.

B.1.   Swing right-hand partner, then left-hand partner.

B.2.   As in " Meeting Six ".

(3)   **Fifth Column Reel**

A.1.   Circle 6 left and right.

A.2.   The men and their right-hand partners do a slantwise right and left through.

B.1.   Balance and swing left partners.

B.2.   Advance, retire and pass through, each man during " retire " raising right arch to pass left girl under, so as to put partners in reversed places for the next round.

THE STAFFORDSHIRE HORNPIPE

SHEPTON HORNPIPE

6

Twenty-one dances from various sources, including squares, contras, long sets, rings and waltzes together with twenty-eight tunes.

Introduction

Edited by
Jack Hamilton

THIS sixth volume of community dances with their loosely associated tunes brings together nearly all the forms which have recently found general favour but have not hitherto been available in print. The notations are, as in the other manuals, sketched in lightly, pre-supposing that the descriptions will be used by those already familiar with community and 'square' dance skills.

The choice of tunes is based on current practice and should be helpful in giving the particular climate of rhythm and style to each individual dance. Other tunes can be found which may be equally satisfactory.

The essence of community dancing lies in its immediate application to the 'layman' who can instantly find an open door to the delights of dancing and to the rich rewards of combining in neighbourly action. The success of this depends directly on an utter simplicity of form. Any degree of complication tends to make the dancer stop and think. Then spontaneity and any flickers of a *new* aliveness are quenched. This is not to suggest that one must be a moron to enjoy 'squares' but rather that the intelligent dancer should learn to develop and use his intuitive sense of movement rather than depend on calculation.

Some of the dance forms in this new manual have been received from traditional practice, others have been 'assembled' by 'callers' in the light of their own experience and preferences. All have something to offer us if we realise that each has its individual method and this method is wedded to the character of the selected music. They have rewarded someone somewhere with pleasure and success. I hope that they continue to do this for many more.

DOUGLAS KENNEDY.

NOTES

1. The particular versions of the airs selected have been established by players of the E.F.D.S.S. which claims copyright except where the source is acknowledged.

2. Tune "Johnny Get Your Hair Cut" is reprinted from "Hill Country Tunes" with kind permission of Prof. Bayard.

3. "Tom Pate" and "Nottingham Swing" reprinted from "Seven Midland Dances" with permission from Sibyl Clark.

4. "Up Jumped The Devil" reprinted by permission of Glad Music Ltd., 38, Soho Square, London, W.1.

5. "Paddy McGinty's Goat" reprinted by permission of Francis, Day and Hunter Ltd., 138–140, Charing Cross Road, London, W.C.2.

6. The assistance of Nan Fleming-Williams in suggesting many of the tunes is acknowledged with thanks.

7. The assistance of Pat Shaw in editing the tunes and suggesting chord symbols is acknowledged with thanks.

8. Permission of Maud Karpeles for tunes taken from Cecil Sharp MSS (Flowers of Edinburgh, Black Jack and Goathland Square Eight) is acknowledged with thanks.

THREE NORTHUMBRIAN DANCES

1. FLOWERS OF EDINBURGH *(North Country variant, contributed by Tony Foxworthy)*

Music   "Flowers of Edinburgh" or any rant tune.

Form   Longways duple proper. Rant step throughout.

A.1.   1st couple dance a figure of eight around 2nd couple. (Finish outside 2nd couple, who turn out, to form line of four.)

A.2.   Reel of four (as in "Soldier's Joy").

B.1.   1st couple, followed by 2nd, lead down the middle; 2nd couple arch, 1st couple under (4 bars). Dance back to places (4 bars).

B.2.   Dance round once and a half (progression).

2. CHEVIOT RANT *(George Mitchell; Billy Miller)*

Music   "Cheviot Rant" or "Storrers" or any rant tune.

Form   Sicilian Circle, couple facing couple. Rant step throughout.

A.1.   Step to contrary (2 bars). Give right hands and change places (2 bars). Repeat facing partner.

A.2.   As A.1.

B.1.   Right hands across, turn out, left hands back.

B.2.   Advance, retire and pass on to the next.

Above contributed by Billy Miller. In its original George Mitchell had the "star" figure preceding the "Waltz Country Dance" figure, i.e.

A.1.   Right and left hands across.

A.2. and B.1.   Changing places in the square.

B.2.   As above.

3. ROXBURGH CASTLE *(Netherton)*

Music   "Roxburgh Castle" or any rant tune.

Form   Longways duple proper.

A.1.   1st and 2nd couples dance round in a circle counter-clockwise (not holding hands) turning single four times as they do so. (Rant or balance step).

A.2.   Right hands across and back (walk step).

B.1.   1st couple lead down the middle and dance back to 2nd couple's place. (Progression).

B.2.   Dance round.

FLOWERS OF EDINBURGH

(Cecil Sharp Mss)

CHEVIOT RANT

(Billy Miller)

STORRERS

ROXBURGH CASTLE

(Traditional)

TWO YORKSHIRE DANCES

4. BLACK JACK *(Submitted by Pat Shaw)*

Music   "Black Jack".

Form   Sicilian Circle, couple facing couple.

A.1.   Clap on first beat and hands four to the left.

A.2.   Clap on first beat and hands four to the right.

B.1.   Bars 1-2.   Partners clap: together, right, together, left.

Bars 3-4.   As bars 1-2 with contrary.

Bars 5-6.   Girls cross over by the left and turn left.
Men cross over by the right and turn right.
(These movements swift and neat).

Bars 7-8.   Repeat bars 5-6 to places.

Bars 9-10. Pass contrary by the right to face next couple.

This dance with tune and figures may be traced back to "Black Joak" in the "Compleat Country Dancing-Master" published by John Walsh in 1731. An astonishing survival of a social dance from the 18th century right down to the present day.

5. GOATHLAND SQUARE EIGHT *(Submitted by Pat Shaw)*

Music   "Goathland Square Eight" (collected with the dance) or any similar reel.

Form   Square set of four couples. Rant step throughout. (Arch figure, A.2., may be walked and pivot step used for the swings).

A.1.   Circle left and right.

A.2.   3rd couple arch, 1st couple under, dance across the set, as in "La Russe", immediately followed by 4th couple arch and 2nd couple under. Repeat to places with 1st and 2nd couples making the arch.

B.1.   Face partner for grand chain half way round the set. Swing partners when you meet.

B.2.   As B.1. to places.

Repeat above ad lib. and finish with

A.   Swing.

B.   Promenade.

A LONG SET DANCE

6. SHEEP'S HILL

Music   "Miller of Stralloch" or any similar jig.

Form   Long set of five or six couples.

A.1.   Top two couples right hands across and back.

A.2.   Top couple galop down the middle and back.

B.1.   Single cast to meet partner at bottom with ballroom hold. All galop up the middle.

B.2.   With same hold and step, double cast to man's left to places. Top couple galop down the middle to bottom place on the last two bars (progression).

(Variation: B.1. may be omitted. Music ABB).

BLACK JACK

(Cecil Sharp Mss)

GOATHLAND SQUARE EIGHT

(Cecil Sharp Mss)

DRUMDELGIE (Miller of Stralloch)

MIDLAND DANCES

7. TOM PATE *(Northamptonshire. Collected by Sibyl Clark)*

Music	"Captain Maguire" or any 32 bar reel.
Form	Progressive double longways. Two couples facing two couples.
A.1.	Lines of four advance and retire twice.
A.2.	Middle four dancers right hands across and back while end dancers swing.
B.1.	Galop with partner (as in "Cumberland Square") sideways passing the couple beside you.
B.2.	Advance and retire with partner. Advance again and pass through to the next four, couples passing down the set making the arch.

8. JOHNNY FETCH YOUR WIFE BACK *(Islip, Northamptonshire)*

Music	"Girl I Left Behind Me" or "The Huntsmen's Chorus"* or "Johnny Get Your Hair Cut" or any 32 bar reel.
Form	Long set for five or six couples.
A.1.	1st and 2nd couples (with right hands crossed) galop down the middle to the bottom. 2nd man galops back with 1st girl (leaving 1st man and 2nd girl at the bottom).
B.1.	Lines advance, retire and cross over.
B.2.	As B.1.
C.1. or A.2.	2nd man galops down the middle with 1st girl, leaves her at the bottom and galops back with his own partner.
C.2. or B.3.	All swing partners. (Commence swing as soon as galoping couple has passed).

Tune "The Huntsmen's Chorus" was collected by Peter Kennedy from Peter Beresford, Oughtershaw, W. Yorks.

9. NOTTINGHAM SWING *(Titchmarsh, one of several variants known in Northamptonshire. Collected by Sibyl Clark)*

Music	"Philibelula All The Way" (see C.D.M.2) or "Paddy McGinty's Goat" or "Kitty O'Neil's Jig" or any similar tune.	
Form	Longways duple proper.	
A.	Bars 1-4.	1st man and 2nd girl link right arms and swing with a step-hop (as in "Drops Of Brandy").
	Bars 5-8.	2nd man and 1st girl the same.
B.	Bars 1-4.	1st couple join inside hands and dance two steps down the middle, turn inwards to face up and cast round the 2nd couple (progression).
	Bars 5-8.	Swing partners (step-hop).

CAPTAIN MAGUIRE

THE HUNTSMEN'S CHORUS

(Collected by Peter Kennedy)

JOHNNY GET YOUR HAIR CUT

(Mrs Armstrong)

PADDY McGINTY'S GOAT

KITTY O'NEIL'S JIG

THREE MIXERS

10. JUBILEE ROUNDABOUT *(Winning entry of Jubilee dance competition submitted by Miss Freda Burford of Ealing with original tunes)*

Music   "Jubilee Roundabout" and second tune.

Form   Big circle. Relaxed and gentle pace recommended.

A.1.   Bars 1-4.   Circle left with rant step.

        Bars 5-8.   Keeping hands, couples turn once round; man backwards, girl forward, with walking step.

A.2.   Circle right and turn as in A.1.

B.1.   Bars 1-2.   Men hand partners in front of them.

        Bars 3-6.   Pousette towards centre and back.

        Bars 7-8.   Keeping right hand to partners left, and raising right arm to pass over his head, men hand partners around and behind them to places.

B.2.   Bars 1-4.   Face partners and with rant step pass each other reluctantly, men passing outside.

        Bars 5-8.   Clap once and do-si-do with new partner with walking step.

11. LUCKY SEVEN *(one of several variants)*

Music   "The Spaceman" or any 32 bar reel or jig.

Form   Big circle.

A.1.   Circle left.

A.2.   All to the middle and back twice.

B.1.   Grand chain.

B.2.   Swing the seventh girl.

12. BIG SET MIXER *(one of many variants)*

Music   "Jimmy Allen" or any 32 bar reel or jig.

Form   Double circle, men facing out.

A.1.   Right hand turn. Left hand turn.

A.2.   Two hand turn. Back to back.

B.1.   Swing next girl on the left (progression).*

B.2.   Promenade.

Progression may be called at other additional points in the dance.

JUBILEE ROUNDABOUT
(Freda Burford, 1961)

Second Tune
(Freda Burford, 1961)

THE SPACEMAN
(Doreen Buckoke, 1961)

JIMMY ALLEN

THREE AMERICAN SET DANCES

13. BUCKSAW REEL *(Becket's Reel) (By Herbie Gaudreau. Holbrook, Mass.)*

Music	"Tipsy Parson" or "Marmaduke's Hornpipe" or 32 bar reel.
Form	Partners side by side in two facing lines. Even number of couples.
A.1.	Allemande left with the girl on the left. (At the end of the line "left" is the other side of the set).*
	Swing partners.
A.2.	Ladies chain with couple opposite.
B.1.	Half right and left through with next couple to the left across the set.**
	Half right and left through with new couple straight across the set (progression).
B.2.	Left hands across and back.

Always with same left hand girl.

**Leaving a neutral couple at each end of the set for this half figure only.*

14. BRIDGE OF ATHLONE

Music	"Rakes of Kildare" or any 32 bar jig.
Form	Long set of five couples.
A.1.	Lines advance, retire and cross over.
A.2.	As A.1.
B.1.	Top couple lead down the middle and back.
B.2.	Top couple cast to make arch at bottom: other couples follow, lead through arch to new places (progression).
A.3.	All arch with partner. Leading girl up the middle and down the outside while leading man up the outside and down the middle.
B.3.	All swing partners.

15. OPERA REEL

Music	"Opera Reel" or any 32 bar reel or jig.
Form	Long set of six couples.
A.1.	Advance and retire. Top couple galop to bottom.
A.2.	Advance and retire. New top couple galop to bottom.
B.1.	Top four circle left and right while middle four right hands across and back and bottom four right and left through.
B.2.	Bottom two couples galop back to top.
	Top couple cast to bottom (progression) while other couples swing.

THE TIPSY PARSON

MARMADUKE'S HORNPIPE

RAKE'S OF KILDARE

OPERA REEL

THREE AMERICAN CONTRAS

16. DEVIL'S DREAM *(Transcribed from an early Ralph Page book)*

Music   "Devil Among The Tailors" or "Up Jumped The Devil" or any other devillish reel.

Form   Longways, duple improper. First couples have crossed over.

A.1.   1st couple down the middle while 2nd couple up the outside. All turn to come back. All give nearest arm to contrary dancer and turn half way.

A.2.   1st couple down the outside while 2nd couple up the middle. All turn to come back. All give left arm to contrary for a full turn into new places (progression).

B.1.   Ladies chain across the set.

B.2.   Half promenade. Half right and left through.

Note: Look well at the contrary dancer before each turn of the dance.

". . . . Again the instruments ended the tune; again they recommenced with as much fire and pathos as if it were the first strain. The air was now that one without any particular beginning, middle, or end, which perhaps, among all the dances which throng an inspired fiddler's fancy, best conveys the idea of the interminable—the celebrated 'Devil's Dream'."

(THOMAS HARDY: "The Return of the Native")

17. FAIRFIELD FANCY *(By Dick Forscher)*

Music   "Farmer's Jamboree" or any 32 bar jig.

Form   Longways, duple improper. First couples have crossed over.

A.1.   Do-si-do contrary. Do-si-do partner.

A.2.   Circle left and back to open out into a line of four with the first couple in the middle, all facing down.

B.1.   Four abreast lead down. 1st couple arch, 2nd couple under (progression). 2nd couple (now facing up) followed by 1st couple (facing down), up the set to new places. (Hands may be held throughout this figure).

B.2.   Ladies chain with next couple. (End couples neutral).

18. GLOVER'S REEL *(By "Duke" Miller. Gloversville, N.Y.)*

Music   "Canadian Breakdown", "Old Countryman's Reel" or any 32 bar reel.

Form   Longways, duple improper. First couples have crossed over.

A.1.   Do-si-do contrary. Allemande right with partner. Allemande left with contrary.

A.2.   Swing partner.

B.1.   1st couple down the middle and back to cast round 2nd couple.

B.2.   Right hands across, left hands back.

UP JUMPED THE DEVIL

(Buck Ryan)

FARMERS' JAMBOREE

CANADIAN BREAKDOWN (McArthur's Reel)

OLD COUNTRYMAN'S REEL

THREE DANCES IN WALTZ TIME

19. MARGARET'S WALTZ *(Composed by Pat Shaw and dedicated to Margaret Grant)*

Music   "Margaret's Waltz" and "Farewell to Devon" played consecutively.

Form   Sicilian Circle. Couple facing couple.

A.1.   Couples advance and retire. Allemande right with contrary.

A.2.   Allemande left with partner. Half Ladies chain.

B.1.   (with contrary girl) Advancing, chassee right (2 bars) and left (2 bars). (Couples are now standing back to back). Turn right into right hands across to original places.

B.2.   Do-si-do contrary. Waltz on with partner.

Note: 8-bar waltz-on may be substituted for B.2.

20. ARMSTRONG'S WALTZ *(John Armstrong)*

Music   "One Night In The Shieling" or "Willie's Drowned In Yarrow" or any 32 bar waltz.

Form   Round set of four couples.

A.1.   Allemande left with the corner (4 bars). Men right hands across in the centre (4 bars).

A.2.   Partners change places giving left hands (2 bars).

Girls right hands across in the centre (4 bars).

Men, giving right hand to partner's left, turn partner under arm into ballroom hold facing round the set (2 bars).

B.1.   Balance (or rock) to man's left and right and waltz on one place.

Balance (or rock) to man's left and right and waltz on one place.

B.2.   Rock left and right again and man waltz on to next partner: waltz her home.

Repeat sequence until meeting original partner.

21. STREETS OF LAREDO *(Singing Square composed by Pat Shaw)*

Music   "Streets of Laredo".

Form *   Square set of four couples. Waltz step throughout.

Introduction   All to the centre and back to your places
      Ladies give right hand and star on your own
    Back with the left hand and turn to your corner
      Left allemande and then right to your own

Chorus   Right to your own and then left to the next one
      And grand right and left just go half the way round
    Waltz your true lover, you waltz home together
      Back to your home in Laredo's fair town

Figure*   The first (2nd etc.) couple waltz down the streets of Laredo
      Divide down the sides and you couple up three
    Up to the centre and back to your places
      Left allemande on the corner lady.

Repeat chorus, then call figure and chorus for 2nd, 3rd and 4th couples. End with introduction and chorus if desired.

*Figure: Leading couple waltz across the set, through the opposite couple, and separate. The girl to stand between the couple originally on her right, the man between the couple originally on his left. Lines of three advance and, the leading couple turning man left and girl right, couples retire to places. All face corners, allemande left and straight into the chorus.

MARGARET'S WALTZ

(Pat Shaw)

FAREWELL TO DEVON

(Pat Shaw)

ONE NIGHT IN THE SHIELING (Way up in Clachan)

WILLIE'S DROWNED IN YARROW

(Original collected by Lucy Broadwood
Adaptation by Pat Shaw)

STREETS OF LAREDO

7

Nineteen dances from various sources including squares, contras, long sets and waltzes together with thirty tunes.

Edited by
Jack Hamilton

1. NORFOLK LONG (SET) DANCE

Contributed by Paul Plumb (Sussex). Collected by Fr. Geo. Chambers from Mrs. Crowfoot of Norfolk in 1932.

Music: "Norfolk Long Dance".

Form: Long set for 6, 8 or 10 couples.

A.1. Right hands across and back in each four.

A.2. Advance and retire twice. Girls inside men's arch, then men between girls.

B.1. Top couple lead down and dance back.

B.2. Top couple swing to bottom place (progression). (The traditional hold for this swing: man supports partner with his hands behind her shoulders while she places her hands on his arms.)

Modern Sussex variant (to any jig) devised by Paul Plumb: B.1. Top couple galop down the middle and up the outside while bottom couple galop up the outside and down the middle. (Separate from but remain facing partner to galop outside.)

2. FOULA REEL

Music: "The Shaalds of Foula" (1) and (2)

Form: Long set of 4 couples.

A.1. and
A.2. 1st couple lead down the middle and "Strip the Willow" up the set.

B.1. 1st couple (man inside) arch over men's line down the set and over girls' line up the set.

B.2. Pousette with partners (one of several variants).
Begin 1st man "pushing", others "pulling", then
1st man pull between 2nd and 3rd couple (other men pushing).
1st man push between 3rd and 4th couple (other men pulling).
1st man pull into bottom place (other men pushing).
(Progression.)

3. KATE'S HORNPIPE

Contributed by Norris Winstone (Norfolk) who first danced this in Yorkshire in 1938.

Music: "The Redesdale Hornpipe" or any lively hornpipe.

Form: Longways.

A.1. 2nd man leads 1st girl down the set with right hand (walking step) while 2nd girl moves up. Turn as a couple, dance back (double step) into new places.

A.2. All face partners, with crossed hands, chassee right (right-close-right-hop) and left. Repeat. Swing partner (double step) finish facing across set with partner on man's right.

B.1. Ladies Chain (as in "Rifleman").

B.2. Swing and change with double step (progression). Finish proper.

NORFOLK LONG DANCE

THE SHAALDS OF FOULA (1)

Collected by Pat Shaw from Gibbie Gray

THE SHAALDS OF FOULA (2)

Collected by Pat Shaw from Mrs. Smith,
10 years school-teacher in Foula

THE REDESDALE HORNPIPE

From Northumbrian Piper's Society Tune Book

4. WALPOLE COTTAGE

Devised by Pat Shaw and commissioned for the farewell party given on 25th May, 1963, to Miss Grace Meikle and Miss Leonie Morris of Walpole Cottage, Chipstead, Surrey.

Music: "Walpole Cottage" Composed by Pat Shaw.

Form: Sicilian Circle threesome.

Introduction: Advance and retire

A. Men turn with right (half way, short arm hold) left to right hand contrary, each other right, left to left hand contrary, each other right, left to left hand partner, each other right, right to right hand partner.

B. Girls right and left hands across.
Right hand girls cast right into reels of three. (Men start right with right hand partner.)

C. Advance, retire. Circle six half way, (progression). Advance, retire. Baskets of three, to face new trio. (Play introduction every time.)

© Pat Shaw

5. THIRD FIGURE JIG

Contributed by Keith Uttley (Kent). Devised by Ron Smedley in 1951, and included with his permission.

Music: "Orcadian Jig" or any well-phrased jig.

Form: Square set.

Introduction:

A. Circle left (slip step).

B. Circle right.

Figure

A.1. 1st couple dance the set (each couple in their turn improvise step and movement).

A.2. 1st couple sashay towards 3rd and back. Sashay forward again to leave 1st girl on left of 3rd man. 1st man to place.

B.1. Threesome forward (2 pas-de-bas steps) and back, forward again, 3rd man turning both girls under, into

B.2. Basket with 1st man.

C.1. 1st and 3rd couples Ladies Chain.

C.2. 1st and 3rd couples promenade inside set to places.

(Repeat figure with each other couple leading.)

Finale

A. Circle left.

B. Promenade.

WALPOLE COTTAGE

Pat Shaw

© Pat Shaw

ORCADIAN JIG

collected by Pat Shaw in Shetland

TWO DANCES FROM THE NORTH

6. THE QUAKER'S WIFE
(Northumberland)

Contributed by Tony Foxworthy.

Music: "Hesleyside Reel" or "Ballantyne's Rant" or any rant.

Form: Longways.

A.1. Set to partners (4 rant steps) and circle left.

A.2. Repeat, circle right.

B.1. 1st couple lead down the middle, followed by 2nd. 2nd couple arch, 1st couple under, to places.

B.2. Dance round once and a half.

(Note: rant step throughout.)

7. DERRY DOWN DERRY
(Cumberland)

Contributed by Tony Foxworthy. Collected by Kathleen Munford, from a Mr. Ryan of Cumberland, in New Zealand and first published in "English Dance and Song" in February, 1941.

Music: "Mr. Sharp's Quadrille" or "Jack's Delight" or any rant.

Form: Long set of four couples, 1st and 2nd improper.

A.1. Circle left and right.

A.2. Straight hey. (1 face 2, 3 face 4.)

B.1. Single cast.

B.2. Double cast. 1st and 3rd to left, 2nd and 4th to right. Come up in lines of four. Leading line turn about to face the following line. (New formation: set now across the room.)

A.3. Square hey in each four. Start with partner; four changes.

A.4. Swing partner. Swing contrary.

B.3. Thread the needle. 1st couple arch, 3rd man leads under.

B.4. Thread the needle. 3rd couple arch, 1st girl leads under.

A.5. Thread the needle. 4th couple arch. 2nd man leads under.

A.6. Thread the needle. 2nd couple arch, 4th girl leads under.

B.5. Square hey (as in A.3.)

B.6. Swing partner. Swing contrary.

A.7. Face down. Double cast. Left four to left, right four to the right, down the middle into original places.

A.8. Face down. Single cast.

B.7. Straight hey (as in A.2.).

B.8. Circle left and right (as in A.1.).

THE HESLEYSIDE REEL

from Northumbrian Piper's Society Tune Book
T. J. Elliott

BALLANTYNE'S RANT

MR. SHARP'S QUADRILLE

From "The Charlton Memorial Tune Book"

JACK'S DELIGHT

TWO DORSETSHIRE DANCES

8. UP THE SIDES AND DOWN THE MIDDLE (Symondsbury)

Contributed by Ann Clayton (Dorset), collected from her father in 1937.

Music: "Up the Sides and Down the Middle" or "The Old Horned Sheep" or any bright jig.

Form: Long set of 4 to 6 (or more) couples.

A.1. Balance twice (hands joined in lines; start onto left foot and swing right leg across) and cross over with polka step.

A.2. Repeat to places.

B.1. 1st couple lead down the middle (inside hands, slowly, with walking step, 8 bars) while 2nd couple lead single cast (polka step) and up through 1st couple's moving arch (progression).

B.2. Swing partners.

9. COLLEGE HORNPIPE

Contributed by Pat Shaw. Transcribed from MSS in Dorchester Museum. Formerly danced in Wessex.

Music: "College Hornpipe" or "The Old Grey Cat" or any reel.

Form: Longways, triple.

A.1. Circle left and back.

A.2. Join inside hands, double cast to the left.

B.1. 1st and 2nd couples lead (or galop) down and back.

B.2. 1st and 2nd couples swing and change once and a half (progression) while 3rd couple swing.

For three-couple set dance, use alternative B.2.:—1st couple swing to bottom while 2nd couple swing on girls' side to top and 3rd couple swing on men's side to middle place.

UP THE SIDES AND DOWN THE MIDDLE

Tune collected by Miss Marjorie Mayne & Peter Kennedy in 1950 from Bert Pidgeon (Melodeon) and Alfie Tuck (Tambourine) of Bridport. Transcribed by Pat Shaw.

THE OLD HORNED SHEEP OR THE HUMOURS OF DONNYBROOK

COLLEGE HORNPIPE

THE OLD GREY CAT

TWO SQUARES

10. WALTZ COTILLON

Contributed by Nibs Matthews—a country version of the Waltz cotillon.

Music: "Cotillon Selection" or any good waltzes.

Form: Square set.

8 Bars Head girls meet, retire and cross over.

8 Bars Side girls the same.

8 Bars Head men the same.

8 Bars Side men the same.

8 Bars Head couples the same.

8 Bars Side couples the same.

16 Bars Waltz chain. (Right to partner, advance, retire, pass with turn (4 bars) left to the next etc.) to places.

8 Bars Lines on head couples (side couples divide to join head couples) advance, retire and cross over.

8 Bars As above, lines on side couples.

8 Bars As above, lines on head couples.

8 Bars As above, lines on side couples.

16 Bars Waltz the set.

11. LA POULE QUADRILLE

Contributed by Roy Dommett (Hampshire). Devised by Jack Hamilton (Kent) 1955.

Music: "La Poule" or any three part jig.

Form: Square set.

A.1. 1st couple dance the set.

A.2. All four couples dance the set.

B.1. Head couples follow M.C.'s call.

B.2. Side couples the same figure.

C.1. Four Ladies Chain.

C.2. Grand Chain* to meet partner. Promenade to place.

(Repeat sequence with 2nd couple leading A.1. and side couples B.1.)

Finale: Swing partners to A. music.

Step smartly into the grand chain.
(Pas-de-bas step recommended with this tune but any step with jig or reel may be used.)

WALTZ COTILLON SELECTION

BABY LIE EASY

Collected by Cyril Tawney
Reproduced by permission of EFDS Publications Ltd.

THE WILD ROVER

heard traditionally
Reproduced by permission of EFDS Publications Ltd.

THE COBBLER

heard traditionally

LA POULE

FOUR CONTRAS

12. JUDGE'S JIG

Contributed by Roy Dommett. A modern New England contra "not for the love-sick or the dull witted". (Judge Charles Merrill, of the Supreme Court of the State of Nevada, 1955.)

Music: "Four & Twenty" or "Ben Chichester" or any reel or jig.

Form: Longways duple improper. 1st couples have crossed over.

A.1. 1st couple down the middle, back, cast one place. (First progression—top couple now neutral.)

A.2. Right hands across and back with the couple below.

B.1. Balance* and swing new contrary (the girl on the left) finish with girl on man's right (second progression).

B.2. Half promenade, half right and left through.

Balance movement is forward and back.

13. SPANKING JACK

Contributed by Jack Hamilton. "Traditional". Introduced by Ricky Holden (Connecticut) at C.S.H., September, 1961. The dance revived by Ralph Page from an early 19th century dance book.

Music: "Sally There's a Bug on Me" or any reel or jig.

Form: Longways duple improper. 1st couples have crossed over.

A.1. Right hands across and back.

A.2. 1st couple down the middle, back and cast round 2nd couple with helping arm (progression).

B.1. 1st couple circle left and right with couple below.

B.2. 1st couple right and left through with couple above.

14. HOMASASSA HORNPIPE

Contributed by Kenneth Clark. Devised by Don Armstrong (Florida, U.S.A.) and included with his permission.

Music: "Jordan" or "Tin Gee Gee" or any reel or jig.

Form: Longways duple improper. 1st couples have crossed over.

A.1. 1st couple do-si-do. Swing contrary and finish with new partner on man's right (progression).

A.2. Half promenade. Half right and left through.

B.1. *Left* hands across and back.

B.2. Ladies Chain.

15. EAST MEETS WEST

Contributed by Nibs Matthews.

Music: "Whose? Jig" or any reel or jig.

Form: Longways duple improper. 1st couples have crossed over.

A.1. 1st couple between 2nd, lead down in line of four. Turn individually to come back to join hands in circle of four. (Progression.)

A.2. Circle left and right.

B.1. Allemande contrary left, partner right, contrary left into position for

B.2. Half promenade, half right and left through.

FOUR AND TWENTY

From COWBOY DANCE TUNES arranged by Fred Knorr to accompany the dances in the book "COWBOY DANCES" by Lloyd Shaw. Book published by the Caxton Printers, Ltd., Caldwell, Idaho, used by permission. (Four and Twenty and Ben Chichester)

BEN CHICHESTER

SALLY THERE'S A BUG ON ME

JORDAN

from Old Familiar Dances
Oliver Ditson
by permission of Theodore Prosser (Alfred A. Kalmus Ltd.)

TIN GEE-GEE (SEVEN-BEAT POLKA)

as played by John Macclosall
Reproduced by permission of Francis, Day & Hunter, Ltd.

WHOSE? JIG

Ken Hillyer

TWO DANCES FROM THE SOUTH

16. SOLDIER'S JOY (Somerset)

Contributed by Hugh Rippon. Collected by Cecil Sharp at Blue Anchor, 1914. (Reproduced by permission of Dr. M. Karpeles.)

Music: "Soldier's Joy", "Sheffield Hornpipe" or any similar reel.

Form: Longways triple.

A.1.   March in a ring to the left to places.

A.2.   Partners advance, bow, turn away to the right and turn each other.

B.1.   1st couple down the middle and back.

B.2.   1st and 2nd couples swing and change (progression). 3rd couple may swing too.

". . . When I had danced a few steps with him he remarked to me 'We've turned round before, both of us'. When I sang the tune from his manuscript book, quite slowly, he said 'That's what I call knocking off the notes'. He spoke of the vicar's wife at Exeter as Lady Warren and said he had danced with all the tip tops out that way . . ."   (CECIL SHARP)

17. HASTE TO THE WEDDING (Sussex and Dorset)

Contributed by Dick Playll (Sussex).

Music: "Haste to the Wedding", "The Champion" or any jig.

Form: Longways.

A.1.   1st couple dance down the set (man outside, girl inside) and back.

A.2.   As A.1. with girl outside and man inside.

B.1.   1st couple circle left (twice or more) with 2nd girl and "pop" her through arch to new place (progression).

B.2.   As B.1. but with 2nd man (progression).

Dorset—notation based on descriptions given in MSS in the Hardy Museum in which the "pop" coincides with the first dotted note and is followed by reversing the circle.

Sussex—the "pop" is usually done at the end of the phrase.

SOLDIER'S JOY
Wm. Winter MSS 1848-50

SHEFFIELD HORNPIPE
from "The Charlton Memorial Tune Book"

HASTE TO THE WEDDING
Hardy Museum MSS

THE CHAMPION

18. QUEEN VICTORIA COUNTRY DANCE

Collected by Dr. T. M. Flett in Dounby, mainland of Orkney, in 1955, and first published in Orkney Herald, October 9, 1956.

Music: "Queen Victoria Country Dance".

Form: Longways proper.

A.1. 1st couple right hand turn, back with the left. Finish between 2nd couple in line of four, girls facing down, men up.

A.2 Balance four in line (4 bars). Turn contrary half round with the right. Girls make an extra half turn. Face down in line of four, arms linked.

B.1. Lead down. Turn towards contrary to come back. 1st couple (on the outside) swing in front to original place.

B.2. Dance round once and a half (flat pas-de-basque) (progression).

Walking step for everything except the balance in A.2. and the Dance Round.

19. THE ROYAL ALBERT

Reprinted from J. F. and T. M. Flett's "Traditional Dancing in Scotland", where further details of steps and style can be found.

Music: "Royal Albert".

Form: Longways, proper.

A 1st couple and 2nd girl basket (pivot step).

B Same three (1st man in the middle) dance down the middle, turn individually, dance back to new places: 1st couple on girls side, 2nd couple on men's side, girls on men's right. (Skip-change step.)

C.1. Quadrille setting to partners (step right, left behind, step right, touch left toe in front). Repeat starting left. Swing partner.

C.2. Ladies Chain with skip-change step and hand turns (not a waist hold).

D Dance round three-quarters (flat pas-de-bas step) (progression).

QUEEN VICTORIA COUNTRY DANCE

from Kerr's collection

ROYAL ALBERT, OR PRINCE OF WALES CONTRE DANCE

(from Köhler's Violin Respositary)

Glossary

by Tony Parkes

NOTE: Many movements are performed with slight variations, depending on the dance and version. Common forms are given here.

THE STEP, unless otherwise specified, is a lively walking step, with the weight kept well forward, over the balls of the feet. Think of pushing back with each foot, rather than reaching ahead.

Above—Toward the top of a longways set.

Advance and retire—*See* Forward and back.

Allemande—A one-hand turn. The name is more American than English and implies a turn in New England style: The dancers are fairly close, with elbows bent, fingers wrapped around each other's hand, and thumbs up.

Arch—Two people join one or both hands and raise their arms to let other dancers through.

Arm right (or arm left)—Link arms with another dancer and dance around each other, usually once.

Back to back—Two facing dancers move around each other, passing right shoulders as they go forward and left shoulders as they back into place. *Compare* Do-si-do.

Balance—Shift body weight onto the right foot, then onto the left, using two beats of music (or one measure of waltz music) for each foot. The usual English balance, called Setting, moves from side to side. In American dances the free foot is often swung across in front, or a forward-and-back motion is used.

Ballroom direction—Counterclockwise around the room.

Ballroom hold—The usual "closed" or "waltz" position: partners facing, man's right arm around woman's back, her left arm resting on his right, her right hand in his left.

Basket—Three or more dancers put arms around each other's waists, hold the hand they find there, and circle clockwise using a pivot step.

Below—Toward the bottom of a longways set.

Big circle—A single circle of couples, all facing the center, woman on her partner's right.

Buzz step—An American name for the pivot step.

Bottom—The end of a longways set farthest from the music.

Cast—In general, to turn away from one's partner and move outside the set. Varies greatly with context. *Compare* Lead.

Chassay (or Chassée)—To move sideward, stepping out with one foot and closing the other to it.

Circle (formation)—*See* Big circle, Progressive circle, Sicilian circle, Double Sicilian circle.

Circle left (or circle right)—Three or more dancers join hands in a ring and move in the direction indicated.

Contra corners—The two people next to one's partner. The first corner is diagonally to the right, the second to the left. *See also* Turn contra corners.

Contra dance—An American term for a progressive longways.

Contrary—In general, the nearest person of opposite sex who is not one's partner. Varies with context.

Corner—In a circle or square set, the woman on the man's left, or the man on the woman's right. *See also* Contra corners.

Cross over—For facing lines, same as Cross right. For facing couples, exchange places with one couple splitting the other.

Cross right (or Cross over by the right)—Change places with someone, passing right shoulders.

Dance round—Same as Swing and change, but often performed with a polka step. *Compare* Waltz on.

Dance the set—One couple, or all the couples, dance once around the set in ballroom direction.

Dip and dive—Couples, holding near hands, dance around a circle (or back and forth in a longways or square set), arching and ducking under by turns. Varies with context.

Do-si-do—An American term for back to back which is becoming more common in English usage.

Double arch—In a line of three, the two on the right make an arch and the one on the left goes under it and around to place, forcing the center dancer to turn under his or her own right arm. Repeat with the left two arching and the right one going under.

Double cast—In a longways set, the top couple cast to one side and the others follow. *Compare* Single cast.

Double Sicilian circle—A progressive circle for groups of four facing four.

Double step—Any "one-two-three" step in which the same foot leads twice, as in the polka step or the rant step.

Down—Toward the bottom of a longways set.

Down the center and back—A common contra dance figure, often followed by a progression in the form of a cast. In some dances partners turn alone, in others they turn as a couple, to return to place. In a few English dances they do not turn at all, but return walking backward.

Down the outside and back—A common contra dance figure, usually beginning with a cast and *not* ending with a progression.

Duple (or Duple minor)—A progressive longways with two couples in each minor set.

Figure eight—Dance through the middle of the set and around contrary, then through the middle and around neighbor on one's own side of the set, while partner does the same. Woman crosses in front of partner each time.

First couple—In a square or a long set dance, the couple nearest the music. In a progressive longways, the couple nearest the music in each minor set (often called "Active couple" or "Actives" in American usage.)

Forward and back—Three steps forward and close the free foot to the other or swing it forward, then three steps backward and close.

Four-handed sets—*See* Duple minor.

Galop—*See* Chassay.

Grand chain—Give right hand to partner, pass by, give left to the next person, and so on around the set for a specified number of hands or until partners are reunited. The usual name in the US is "Grand right and left."

Grand circle—*See* Big circle.

Half promenade—Two facing couples exchange places by promenading across, keeping to the right, and wheeling to face the other couple again.

Hands four—A circle of four, a duple minor set, or the procedure for forming such a set (dancers take hands in groups of four, beginning at the top).

Heads—An American term for tops.

Hey (or straight hey)—Same as Reel of three or Reel of four. *See also* Square hey.

Honor—A bow or curtsy, its formality or lack thereof depending heavily on context.

Hornpipe—A tune in fairly slow $\frac{4}{4}$ time with a dotted rhythm, lending itself to step-hops and slow polka steps.

Improper—Of a couple, having the man on the woman's side and vice versa. Of a dance, beginning with the first couples standing thus. *Compare* proper.

Jig—A tune in $\frac{6}{8}$ time, giving a bouncy feeling to the dance.

Ladies chain—Women of two facing couples join right hands, pass by each other, and join left hands with the opposite man (in a longways this is usually original partner). He assists her in turning to face the other couple, sometimes putting his right arm around her waist. That progression is often called a "Half chain"; it is usually repeated to starting places.

Lead—In general, to take one's partner by the hand and move inside the set. Varies greatly with context. *Compare* Cast.

Leading couple—The couple whose turn it is to initiate the figure (generally called "Active couple" in American usage).

Long set—A longways dance. The name implies a set dance rather than a progressive one.

Longways—The most common English country-dance formation. A line of men faces a line of women, 5 or 6 feet apart, with each dancer facing partner. For further description, *see* Progressive longways; Set dance; Proper; Improper.

Minor set—In a progressive longways, the two or three couples working together in each round.

Mixer—A dance in which partners change permanently.

Neighbor—The person on one's own side of a minor set.

Opposite—In a square or progressive circle, the person directly facing one.

Pas-de-bas (or Pas-de-basque)—In English dancing, similar to a polka step, though it has many variations in other countries. Can be performed in place (as a form of setting), while traveling forward or backward, or while turning as a couple in ballroom hold.

Pass through—An American term for Cross right.

Partner—In a square or circle, the woman on the man's right, or the man on the woman's left. In nearly all longways, partners face one another to start.

Pivot step—In a swing or a basket, dancers revolve clockwise as a couple or group by stepping on the right foot and pushing back with the left, keeping body weight over the right foot. Called "Buzz step" in American usage.

Polka step—A "one-two-three" step in which (for example) the left foot takes body weight, the right closes to it briefly, and the left takes weight again (step-close-step). The fourth count is a pause, often with a small lift or hop as a lead-in to the next step. Usually men start on the left foot, women on the right.

Polka swing—Same as Dance round.

Pousette—Partners, facing and holding both hands, take turns pushing and pulling one another. Can be performed as a figure in itself (like Forward and back) or a means of progression (Couples around each other).

Progression—The change of partners in a mixer or couples in a progressive dance, or the point at which the change occurs. This is sometimes pointed out in the dance descriptions where it may not be obvious.

Progressive circle—A dance in which couples (or groups of three or four) are arranged like the spokes of a wheel around the room, facing in alternate directions. Facing couples or groups dance together, then move around or through each other to meet a new group.

Progressive longways—A dance "for as many as will" in which the set is divided into minor sets of two or three couples, who dance together for one round. During the round, the first couple in each minor set moves down the line one place, ready to dance with the next one or two couples below them. Couples reaching the top or bottom wait one round (in a duple) and start progressing the other way, with new numbers. *See* Triple minor for that form's extra rules; *compare* Set dance.

Promenade—Couples dance in ballroom direction around the set. Partners are side by side, with hands crossed in front or with left hands joined in front of the man and his right arm around the woman's waist. The second hold is more common in New England.

Proper—Of a couple, standing with the man on the caller's right and the woman on the caller's left. Of a dance, beginning with all couples standing thus. *Compare* improper.

Quadrille—A dance in square formation.

Rant—A tune in moderate $\frac{2}{4}$ time, faster than a hornpipe but slower than a reel.

Rant step—A deliberate polka step, usually with a slight leap onto each foot and the three steps given more equal weight than in a standard polka. When the rant step is used solo (in place or traveling), the front foot usually taps twice before taking body weight on the third count (tap-tap-change).

Reel—The most common type of tune, in fast $\frac{2}{4}$ time, lending itself to a brisk walking step.

Reel of four—A weaving figure. Four dancers in line pass alternate shoulders, making loops at the ends before coming back in with the shoulder they last used. Can begin with the two center dancers facing each other or the ends.

Reel of three—Similar to Reel of four. Two dancers start while the third hangs back for a couple of counts; after the end loop, each dancer comes back in between the other two.

Right and left through—Two facing couples exchange places, each dancer passing right shoulders with the opposite (in a longways, this is usually the original partner). Couples then wheel to face each other again, the man going backward and the woman forward. This turn is performed side-by-side in New England promenade hold, or with only left hands joined, or with arms around waists, or without touching at all. This progression is sometimes called "Half right and left"; it is often repeated to starting places ("Right and left back"). The roundtrip is called simply "Right and left." Can be done by two men facing two women; the person on the left backs up during the turn.

Right hands across—Four dancers extend right arms so that each pair of diagonally facing dancers can join right hands, one pair crossing over the other. They move around in the direction they face (clockwise). On the call "Left hands back," they change hands and go the other way. In America, this is usually called "Right-hand star" and often danced with each dancer holding the wrist of the one ahead.

Sashay—*See* Chassay.

Schottische—A tune in slow dotted $\frac{4}{4}$ time, similar to the hornpipe and sometimes used for country dances in hornpipe rhythm.

Set (verb)—To balance from side to side, either in place or while moving forward. Usual footwork is to shift weight onto the right foot, moving slightly to one's right with a "one-two-three" (quick changes of weight), then repeat to one's left.

Set dance—A longways with a prescribed number of couples in which only one couple at a time is active. At the end of its round, the first couple moves to the bottom and the new top couple becomes the first couple. *Compare* Progressive longways, in which couples keep their numbers through several rounds.

Sicilian circle—A progressive circle in which one couple facing clockwise dances with another couple facing counterclockwise.

Sides—The couples in a square who have the music to their right or left. *Compare* Tops.

Single cast—In a longways set, dancers turn away from their partners and move solo, usually down the outside. *Compare* Double cast.

Single step—The ordinary walking step. *Compare* Double step.

Single turn—A rare name for a one-hand turn. Not to be confused with turn single.

Skip-change step—A polka-like step borrowed from Scottish country dancing, where it is performed according to precise rules. In English dancing, a vigorous polka step will suffice, performed with plenty of forward movement and none to the side.

Square hey—Four dancers execute a miniature grand chain around the edge of their minor set. Also known as "Circular hey" or "Rights and lefts"; called "Square through" in modern American usage.

Square set—Four couples stand one on each side of a square, 6 to 8 feet across. Woman is on her partner's right.

Star—*See* Right hands across.

Step-hop—Step on one foot, hop on it, then repeat on other foot.

Stepping—A rant step or polka step, performed in place or while traveling.

Straight hey—*See* Reel or four or Reel of three.

Strip the willow—In a set dance, first couple link right arms and dance once or once-and-a-half around until they face the line of opposite sex. Each turns the first person in that line by the left elbow, partner by the right, next in line by the left, and so on until all have been turned. Occasionally danced starting left.

Swing—Two dancers in ballroom hold revolve clockwise with a pivot step. To avoid tripping, each dancer keeps own feet to the left of partner's feet, so that partner is on a slight diagonal to the right. Motion is more forward than sideward.

Swing and change—Two couples, each in ballroom hold, exchange places by moving past each other (or, if time permits, going once-and-a-half around each other), using a pivot step or a polka step. *Compare* Dance round; Waltz on.

Thread the needle—From a circle, designated person releases one hand and leads the other dancers through an arch (usually made by the person he or she broke with and that person's neighbor).

Top—The end of a longways set nearest the music.

Top couple—The couple nearest the music. In a set dance, same as first couple; in a progressive longways, the couple about to begin their journey down the line as a first couple.

Tops—In a square, the couples with their backs to the music or facing the music. Called "Heads" in American usage.

Triple (or Triple minor)—A progressive longways with three couples in each minor set. Inactive couples alternate between being second and third couples. Incomplete minor sets dance with an imaginary third couple (at the bottom) or wait till complete (at the top).

Turn—In general, two dancers join right (or left) hands about shoulder-high with elbows slightly bent, and dance around each other, "giving weight" (that is, pulling gently but firmly away from each other).

Turn contra corners—Active couples turn partner by the right hand, first contra corner by the left, partner by the right, and second contra corner by the left. Note that this figure is described but not named in "Chorus Jig" and "Sackett's Harbor," and that an allemande hold, not an elbow swing, is traditionall in these American dances (the figure name is also traditional).

Turn single—Turn solo, to the right, in a very small circle for four steps, returning to place. *Compare* Single turn.

Two-step—A smooth polka step without the hop.

Two-step "waltz"—The word "waltz" refers to the traffic pattern, not the step, which is a turning two-step in ballroom hold and direction.

Up—Toward the top of a longways set.

Waltz on—*Same as* Swing and change, but performed in waltz time.

Waltz the set—*Same as* Dance the set, performed in waltz time.

Whole set—*See* Set dance.

Bibliography and Discography

NOTE: Many of these titles are published by special interest groups with broad aims and small budgets. A particular title may be unavailable for some months while remaining officially "in print." When a book or record is in fact deleted, another publisher may obtain reprint rights or a similar title serving the same purpose may appear. It is wise to obtain the current catalogues of the major sources in the field. A key to the publishers, with their addresses, appears at the end of this section.

BOOKS

Traditional English Country Dancing

English Folk Dancing in Primary School (Novello)

Callers' Choice, Books 1 and 2 (EFDSS)

Clark, Sibyl, *Swing Partners* (Novello)

Everyday Dances (EFDSS)

Gadd, May, *Country Dances of Today,* Volumes 1 and 2 (CDSSA)

Captains Ceilidh

Historical English Country Dancing

Apted Book of Country Dances (EFDSS)

Playford, John, *The English Dancing Master* (reprint of 1650 edition, with tunes in modern musical notation) (PBC)

Sharp, Cecil, *The Country Dance Book* (6 volumes, reprinted in 3 volumes) (HS)

Van Cleef, Frank, *24 Dances from the Playford Editions* (PBC)

New England Square and Contra Dancing

Armstrong, Don, *The Caller/Teacher Manual for Contras* (SIO)

Jennings, Larry, *Zesty Contras* (NEFFA)

Page, Ralph, *An Elegant Collection of Contras and Squares* (LSF)

——— *Heritage Dances of Early America* (LSF)

——— *The Ralph Page Book of Contras* (EFDSS)

Sannella, Ted, *Balance and Swing* (CDSSA)

Tolman, Beth, and Ralph Page, *The Country Dance Book* (out of print)

Other Traditional American Styles

Dalsemer, Bob, *West Virginia Square Dances* (CDSSA)

Napier, Patrick, *Kentucky Mountain Square Dancing* (available from LSF)

Shaw, Lloyd, *Cowboy Dances* (available from LSF)

——— *The Round Dance Book* (available from LSF)

RECORDS

Traditional English Country Dancing

(all by EFDSS, available from CDSSA)

BR 1, *Barn Dance*

BR 2, *Barn Dance Two*

BR 3, *English Folk Dancing in the Primary School*

BR 4, *Callers' Choice*

BR 5, *English Country Dances for Young Folk*

BR 6, *Flowers and Frolics*

BR 7, *Captains Ceilidh*

CDM Series, *Dances from Community Dances Manual* (keyed to this book) Cassette TC EMS 1387 (EMI)

Historical English Country Dancing

CDS 6, *By Popular Demand* (CDSSA)

CDS 7, *Claremont Country Dance Band* (CDSSA)

CDS 8, *Step Stately* (CDSSA)

CDS 9, *Juice of Barley* (CDSSA)

LIB 1&2, *Apted Country Dances* (2 volumes, EFDSS)

LIB 1 2 & 3, *Apted Country Dances* (3 volumes, EFDSS)

PLA 1–4, *The English Dancing Master* (4 volumes, EFDSS)

VR 013, *Bare Necessities* (Varrick Records, a division of Rounder Records)

New England Square and Contra Dancing

FR 200a, *Kitchen Junket* (Alcazar; FR 200b is the same record with calls)

FR 201, *Maritime Dance Party* (Alcazar)

FR 203, 204, *New England Chestnuts 1 & 2* (Alcazar)

F&W 6, *Square Dance Tunes for a Yankee Caller* (F&W Records)

Other Traditional American Styles

AR 52, *Big Circle Mountain Square Dancing* (Activity Records; with calls)

AR 53, *Appalachian Clog Dancing* (Activity Records)

AR 82, *Mountain Dance Music Comes Alive* (Activity Records)

FF 237, *Clogging Lessons* (Flying Fish Records)

FLK LP-36, *Big Circle Mountain Dance Music* (Folkraft Records)

FR 202, *Potluck and Dance Tonite* (Alcazar; with calls)

SOURCES

Activity Records, P.O. Box 392, Freeport, NY 11520

Alcazar, P.O. Box 429, Waterbury, VT 05676

Andy's Front Hall, Drawer A, Voorheesville, NY 12186

CDSSA: Country Dance and Song Society of America, 17 New South Street, Northampton, MA 01060

EFDSS: English Folk Dance and Song Society, 2 Regent's Park Road, London NW1 7AY, England (in US order from CDSSA)

F&W Records, P.O. Box 12, Plymouth, VT 05056

Flying Fish Records, 1304 West Schubert, Chicago, IL 60614

Folkraft Records, 10 Fenwick St., Newark, NJ 07114

HS: H. Styles, 5 Beddington Gardens, Carshalton, Surrey 8MS 3HL, UK

LSF: Lloyd Shaw Foundation, P.O. Box 1148, Salida, CO 81201

NEFFA: New England Folk Festival Association, 595 Massachusetts Ave., Room 210, Cambridge, MA 02139

PBC: Princeton Book Company, Publishers, P.O. Box 109, Princeton, NJ 08542

Rounder Records, One Camp St., Cambridge, MA 02140

SIO: Sets in Order, American Square Dance Society, 462 North Robertson, Los Angeles, CA 90048

Index

Dances

Tunes

The English Folk Dance and Song Society
President: H.R.H. The Princess Margaret

- Is a registered charity supported by several thousand members.
- Is trustee of Cecil Sharp House, England's National Folk Centre.
- Stimulates the practice and enjoyment of folk music, dance, song, custom and drama.
- Organises thousands of dances, concerts and ceilidhs each year through its national network of clubs, district and area committees.
- Maintains a list of clubs and of related events.
- Publishes books and records covering all aspects of our traditions.
- Owns the unique Vaughan Williams Memorial Library containing over 11,000 books and 3000 recordings.
- Through the VWML, provides facilities, help and advice to collectors and those researching our folk heritage.
- Enables people to learn more about our folk traditions and become more proficient in their use through training courses, workshops, lectures and classes.
- Advises and has close association with many other organisations.
- Supports and encourages traditional artists.
- Organises comprehensive year-round programme of folk activity at Cecil Sharp House.

There is a wealth of interest to be had from becoming a member of the EFDSS. Why not join us?

Write for more information to:

◆

The English Folk Dance and Song Society
Cecil Sharp House, 2 Regent's Park Road,
London NW1 7AY
Telephone 071-485 2206